FASHION ACCESSORIES

MODEACCESSOIRES
ACCESSORI MODA
ACCESSOIRES DE MODE
ACCESORIOS DE MODA
ACESSÓRIOS DE MODA
ファッション・アクセサリー
时尚饰品

THE PEPIN PRESS

AMSTERDAM & SINGAPORE

The Pepin Press
P.O. Box 10349
1001 EH Amsterdam
T +31 20 4202021
F +31 20 4201152
mail@pepinpress.com
www.pepinpress.com

Concept & design: Pepin van Roojen
Project management & layout: Femke van Eijk
Production assistant: Kirsten Quast
Text & captions: Femke van Eijk (edited by Ros Horton)
Translations: LocTeam (English, German, Italian, French, Spanish, Portuguese),
Michie Yamakawa (Japanese), The Big Word (Chinese)

ISBN 978 90 5496 058 4

10 9 8 7 6 5 4 3 2 1

2010 09 08 07 06

Printed in Singapore

FASHION ACCESSORIES

MODEACCESSOIRES
ACCESSORI MODA
ACCESSOIRES DE MODE
ACCESORIOS DE MODA
ACESSÓRIOS DE MODA
ファッション・アクセサリー
时尚饰品

THE PEPIN PRESS
AMSTERDAM & SINGAPORE

Contents

Inhaltsverzeichnis

Indice

Contenu

Índice

Índice

目次

目录

Introduction

Whether for functional or purely decorative purposes, accessories have been used all over the world since ancient times. This book offers a wide selection of images of items used to adorn the body or complement one's attire, starting with items used to decorate the head (hats, crowns, diadems, etc.) and face (nose and earrings, etc.), and works its way down the body through, among other things, collars, shawls and belts to shoes and footwear. Naturally, it also contains images of bags, purses, umbrellas and fans, as well as all conceivable forms of jewellery.

On pages 379–390 you will find short descriptions (in English) of each picture.

Einleitung

Ob funktional oder rein dekorativ, Accessoires werden bereits seit dem Altertum auf der ganzen Welt verwendet. Dieses Buch bietet eine große Auswahl an Bildern von Gegenständen, die zur Verzierung des Körpers oder zur Ergänzung der Kleidung dienen. Es beginnt mit verschiedenen Arten von Kopfschmuck (Hüten, Kronen, Diademen etc.) sowie Gesichtsschmuck (Nasen- und Ohrringen etc.) und wandert am Körper entlang, wobei es unter anderem Kolliers, Tücher, Gürtel und Schuhwerk behandelt. Natürlich sind auch Bilder von Taschen, Geldbörsen, Schirmen und Fächern sowie von allen erdenklichen Schmuckstücken enthalten.

Auf den Seiten 379–390 finden Sie kurze Beschreibungen (auf Englisch) zu jedem Bild.

Introduzione

Gli accessori sono stati sempre utilizzati fin dall'antichità in tutto il mondo, sia come soluzione funzionale sia a scopo puramente decorativo. Il volume offre una ricca selezione di fotografie di oggetti ornamentali o complementi per abbigliamento, a partire da quelli utilizzati per abbellire il capo (cappelli, corone, diademi) e il volto (orecchini, anche da naso), passando, tra gli altri, a scialli, collane e cinture, per finire alle calze e calzature. Naturalmente, non potevano mancare borse, sacche, ombrelli e ventagli, come anche tutte le forme possibili di gioielli.

Alle pagine 379–390 sono riportate le didascalie (in inglese) che descrivono sinteticamente l'oggetto di ogni fotografia.

Introduction

Que ce soit dans un but fonctionnel ou simplement pour décorer, les accessoires ont de tout temps été utilisés dans le monde entier. Cet ouvrage vous présente une importante sélection d'images de différents objets utilisés pour embellir le corps ou en complément des vêtements; depuis les coiffures (chapeaux, couronnes, diadèmes, etc.) et les objets destinés à orner le visage (bijoux de nez, boucles d'oreille, etc.) jusqu'à ceux utilisés pour le corps comme, par exemple, les cols, les châles, les ceintures ou encore les chaussures. Il contient évidemment des images de sacs, de porte-monnaie, de parapluies et d'éventails, mais aussi de tout type de bijoux.

Vous trouverez aux pages 379–390 une brève description de chaque image (en anglais).

Introducción

La utilización de accesorios de moda, tanto funcionales como puramente decorativos, es una práctica habitual en todo el mundo desde tiempos remotos. En este libro se ofrece una amplia selección de imágenes de todo tipo de artículos empleados para adornar el cuerpo y complementar la indumentaria: desde los accesorios que sirven para decorar la cabeza (sombreros, coronas, diademas, etc.) y la cara (pendientes, anillos de nariz, etc.) hasta los que cubren los pies (zapatos y otro tipo de calzado), pasando por el resto del cuerpo (cuellos, chales y cinturones, entre muchos otros). Y, naturalmente, se incluyen imágenes de bolsos, monederos, paraguas y abanicos, así como de todas las formas imaginables de joyas.

Las páginas 379–390 contienen breves descripciones (en inglés) de cada imagen.

Introdução

Quer cumpram funções específicas ou sirvam apenas para fins decorativos, desde tempos imemoriais que se usam acessórios em todo o mundo. Este livro proporciona uma ampla selecção de imagens de artigos usados para adornar o corpo ou complementar a indumentária, começando pelos artigos usados para embelezar a cabeça (chapéus, coroas, diademas, etc.) e o rosto (brincos para o nariz e orelhas, etc.), passando pelos colares, xailes e cintos, e acabando nos sapatos e outro calçado. Como não podia deixar de ser, contém imagens de malas, bolsas, chapéus-de-chuva e leques, bem como de todas as formas possíveis de joalharia.

Nas páginas 379–390, são fornecidas breves descrições (em inglês) de cada imagem.

序文

目的が機能であれ、装飾であれ、アクセサリーは、古代から世界中で使われてきました。本書には、ボディの美しさを強調したり、装いの一部のために使用されてきた数々のアイテムを収録しています。掲載しているアクセサリーには、帽子や王冠、髪飾り、鼻飾りやイヤリング、襟飾り、ショール、ベルト、靴、バッグ、財布、傘、扇、ジュエリーなどが含まれます。

379~390ページには、各写真についての短い説明（英語）が載っています。

简介

从远古时代起，饰品就在世界各地广泛使用，或用于某种功能，或纯粹用于装饰。本书中提供了丰富的身体饰品或服装饰品图片，从头饰（帽子、皇冠、头带等）到脸部饰品（鼻饰和耳环等），以及用于身体各个部位的饰品，包括项饰、披肩、皮带、鞋袜等。当然，本书中还收录了许多包、钱包、伞和扇子的图片，以及您所能想象到的各种珠宝图片。

在第 379-390 页中，您可以找到每张图片的简短说明（英文）。

crowns • Kronen • corone • couronnes • coronas • coroas • 王冠 • 皇冠

crowns • Kronen • corone • couronnes • coronas • coroas • 王冠 • 皇冠

crowns • Kronen • corone • couronnes • coronas • coroas • 王冠 • 皇冠

crowns • Kronen • corone • couronnes • coronas • coroas • 王冠 • 皇冠

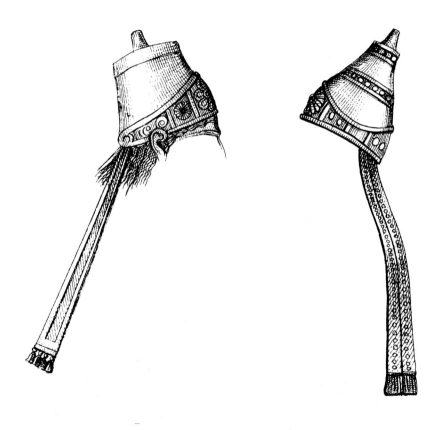

crowns • Kronen • corone • couronnes • coronas • coroas • 王冠 • 皇冠

crowns • Kronen • corone • couronnes • coronas • coroas • 王冠 • 皇冠

crowns • Kronen • corone • couronnes • coronas • coroas • 王冠 • 皇冠

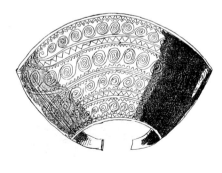

crowns • Kronen • corone • couronnes • coronas • coroas • 王冠 • 皇冠

crowns • Kronen • corone • couronnes • coronas • coroas • 王冠 • 皇冠

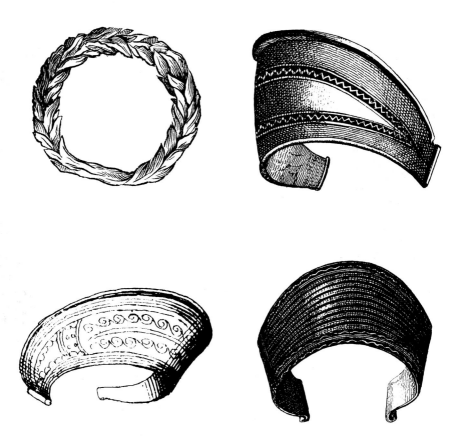

crowns • Kronen • corone • couronnes • coronas • coroas • 王冠 • 皇冠

helmets • Helme • copricapo • casques • cascos • capacetes • ヘルメット • 头盔

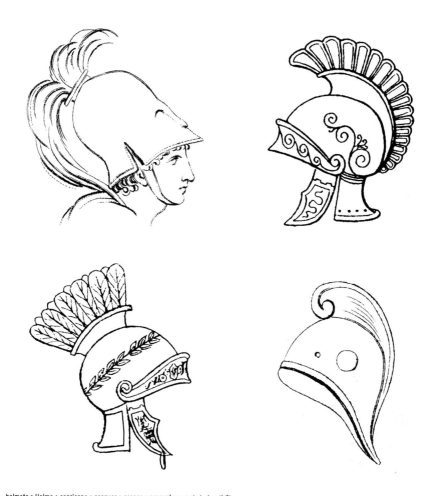

helmets • Helme • copricapo • casques • cascos • capacetes • ヘルメット • 头盔

helmets • Helme • copricapo • casques • cascos • capacetes • ヘルメット • 头盔

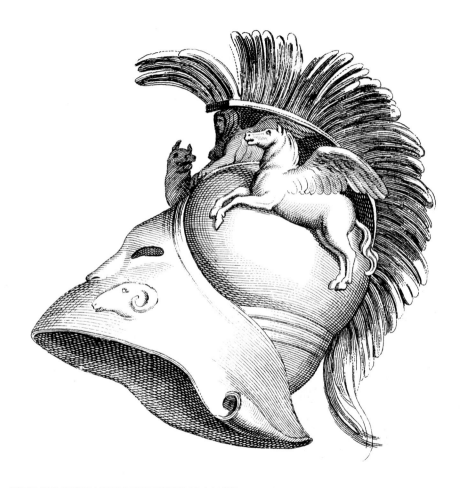

helmets • Helme • copricapo • casques • cascos • capacetes • ヘルメット • 头盔

crowns • Kronen • corone • couronnes • coronas • coroas • 王冠 • 皇冠

crowns • Kronen • corone • couronnes • coronas • coroas • 王冠 • 皇冠

crowns • Kronen • corone • couronnes • coronas • coroas • 王冠 • 皇冠

crowns • Kronen • corone • couronnes • coronas • coroas • 王冠 • 皇冠

crowns • Kronen • corone • couronnes • coronas • coroas • 王冠 • 皇冠

crowns • Kronen • corone • couronnes • coronas • coroas • 王冠 • 皇冠

crowns • Kronen • corone • couronnes • coronas • coroas • 王冠 • 皇冠

crowns • Kronen • corone • couronnes • coronas • coroas • 王冠 • 皇冠

crowns • Kronen • corone • couronnes • coronas • coroas • 王冠 • 皇冠

crowns • Kronen • corone • couronnes • coronas • coroas • 王冠 • 皇冠

crowns • Kronen • corone • couronnes • coronas • coroas • 王冠 • 皇冠

crowns • Kronen • corone • couronnes • coronas • coroas • 王冠 • 皇冠

crowns • Kronen • corone • couronnes • coronas • coroas • 王冠 • 皇冠

crowns • Kronen • corone • couronnes • coronas • coroas • 王冠 • 皇冠

crowns • Kronen • corone • couronnes • coronas • coroas • 王冠 • 皇冠

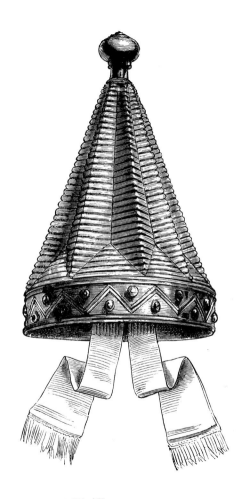

crowns • Kronen • corone • couronnes • coronas • coroas • 王冠 • 皇冠

42

crowns • Kronen • corone • couronnes • coronas • coroas • 王冠 • 皇冠

crowns • Kronen • corone • couronnes • coronas • coroas • 王冠 • 皇冠

crowns • Kronen • corone • couronnes • coronas • coroas • 王冠 • 皇冠

crowns • Kronen • corone • couronnes • coronas • coroas • 王冠 • 皇冠

46

crowns • Kronen • corone • couronnes • coronas • coroas • 王冠 • 皇冠

crowns • Kronen • corone • couronnes • coronas • coroas • 王冠 • 皇冠

hats • Hüte • cappelli • chapeaux • sombreros • chapéus • 帽子 • 帽子

hats • Hüte • cappelli • chapeaux • sombreros • chapéus • 帽子 • 帽子

hats • Hüte • cappelli • chapeaux • sombreros • chapéus • 帽子 • 帽子

hats • Hüte • cappelli • chapeaux • sombreros • chapéus • 帽子 • 帽子

hats • Hüte • cappelli • chapeaux • sombreros • chapéus • 帽子 • 帽子

hats • Hüte • cappelli • chapeaux • sombreros • chapéus • 帽子 • 帽子

hats • Hüte • cappelli • chapeaux • sombreros • chapéus • 帽子 • 帽子

hats • Hüte • cappelli • chapeaux • sombreros • chapéus • 帽子 • 帽子

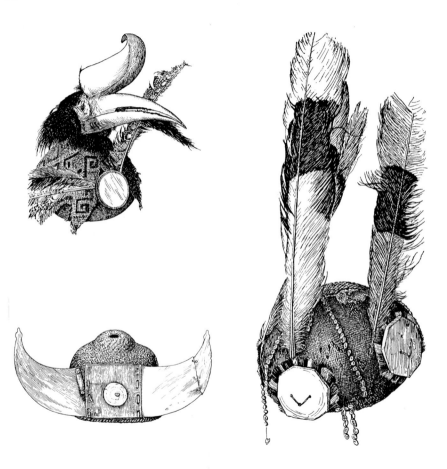

hats • Hüte • cappelli • chapeaux • sombreros • chapéus • 帽子 • 帽子

hats • Hüte • cappelli • chapeaux • sombreros • chapéus • 帽子 • 帽子

hats • Hüte • cappelli • chapeaux • sombreros • chapéus • 帽子 • 帽子

hats • Hüte • cappelli • chapeaux • sombreros • chapéus • 帽子 • 帽子

hats • Hüte • cappelli • chapeaux • sombreros • chapéus • 帽子 • 帽子

hats • Hüte • cappelli • chapeaux • sombreros • chapéus • 帽子 • 帽子

hats • Hüte • cappelli • chapeaux • sombreros • chapéus • 帽子 • 帽子

hats • Hüte • cappelli • chapeaux • sombreros • chapéus • 帽子 • 帽子

hats • Hüte • cappelli • chapeaux • sombreros • chapéus • 帽子 • 帽子

hats • Hüte • cappelli • chapeaux • sombreros • chapéus • 帽子 • 帽子

hats • Hüte • cappelli • chapeaux • sombreros • chapéus • 帽子 • 帽子

hats • Hüte • cappelli • chapeaux • sombreros • chapéus • 帽子 • 帽子

hats • Hüte • cappelli • chapeaux • sombreros • chapéus • 帽子 • 帽子

hats • Hüte • cappelli • chapeaux • sombreros • chapéus • 帽子 • 帽子

hats • Hüte • cappelli • chapeaux • sombreros • chapéus • 帽子 • 帽子

hats • Hüte • cappelli • chapeaux • sombreros • chapéus • 帽子 • 帽子

hats • Hüte • cappelli • chapeaux • sombreros • chapéus • 帽子 • 帽子

hats • Hüte • cappelli • chapeaux • sombreros • chapéus • 帽子 • 帽子

hats • Hüte • cappelli • chapeaux • sombreros • chapéus • 帽子 • 帽子

hats • Hüte • cappelli • chapeaux • sombreros • chapéus • 帽子 • 帽子

hats • Hüte • cappelli • chapeaux • sombreros • chapéus • 帽子 • 帽子

hats • Hüte • cappelli • chapeaux • sombreros • chapéus • 帽子 • 帽子

hats • Hüte • cappelli • chapeaux • sombreros • chapéus • 帽子 • 帽子

hats • Hüte • cappelli • chapeaux • sombreros • chapéus • 帽子 • 帽子

hats • Hüte • cappelli • chapeaux • sombreros • chapéus • 帽子 • 帽子

hats • Hüte • cappelli • chapeaux • sombreros • chapéus • 帽子 • 帽子

veils • Schleier • veli • voiles • velos • véus • ベール • 面纱

veils • Schleier • veli • voiles • velos • véus • ベール • 面纱

veils • Schleier • veli • voiles • velos • véus • ベール • 面纱

veils • Schleier • veli • voiles • velos • véus • ベール • 面纱

veils • Schleier • veli • voiles • velos • véus • ベール • 面纱

veils • Schleier • veli • voiles • velos • véus • ベール • 面纱

veils • Schleier • veli • voiles • velos • véus • ベール • 面纱

veils • Schleier • veli • voiles • velos • véus • ベール • 面纱

veils • Schleier • veli • voiles • velos • véus • ベール • 面纱

veils • Schleier • veli • voiles • velos • véus • ベール • 面纱

veils • Schleier • veli • voiles • velos • véus • ベール • 面纱

veils • Schleier • veli • voiles • velos • véus • ベール • 面纱

veils • Schleier • veli • voiles • velos • véus • ベール • 面纱

veils • Schleier • veli • voiles • velos • véus • ベール • 面纱

veils • Schleier • veli • voiles • velos • véus • ベール • 面纱

veils • Schleier • veli • voiles • velos • véus • ベール • 面纱

veils • Schleier • veli • voiles • velos • véus • ベール • 面纱

veils • Schleier • veli • voiles • velos • véus • ベール • 面纱

veils • Schleier • veli • voiles • velos • véus • ベール • 面纱

veils • Schleier • veli • voiles • velos • véus • ベール • 面纱

veils • Schleier • veli • voiles • velos • véus • ベール • 面纱

veils • Schleier • veli • voiles • velos • véus • ベール • 面纱

veils • Schleier • veli • voiles • velos • véus • ベール • 面纱

veils • Schleier • veli • voiles • velos • véus • ベール • 面纱

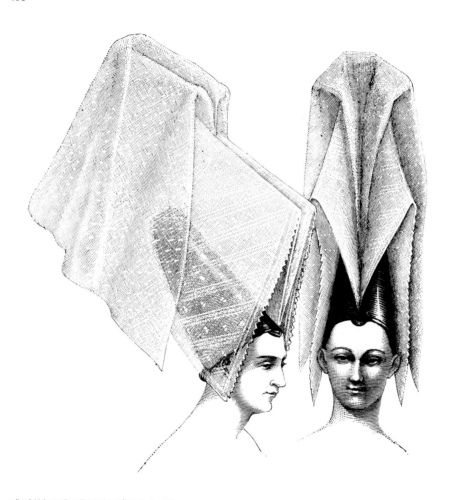

veils • Schleier • veli • voiles • velos • véus • ベール • 面纱

veils • Schleier • veli • voiles • velos • véus • ベール • 面纱

veils • Schleier • veli • voiles • velos • véus • ベール • 面纱

veils • Schleier • veli • voiles • velos • véus • ベール • 面纱

veils • Schleier • veli • voiles • velos • véus • ベール • 面纱

veils • Schleier • veli • voiles • velos • véus • ベール • 面纱

veils • Schleier • veli • voiles • velos • véus • ベール • 面纱

veils • Schleier • veli • voiles • velos • véus • ベール • 面纱

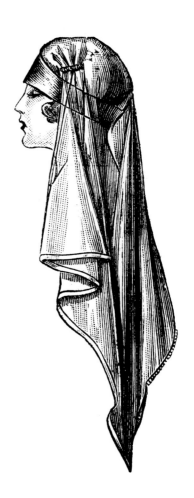

veils • Schleier • veli • voiles • velos • véus • ベール • 面纱

veils • Schleier • veli • voiles • velos • véus • ベール • 面纱

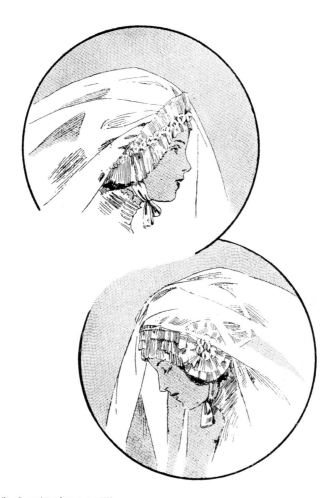

veils • Schleier • veli • voiles • velos • véus • ベール • 面纱

hats • Hüte • cappelli • chapeaux • sombreros • chapéus • 帽子 • 帽子

hats • Hüte • cappelli • chapeaux • sombreros • chapéus • 帽子 • 帽子

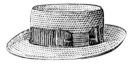

hats • Hüte • cappelli • chapeaux • sombreros • chapéus • 帽子 • 帽子

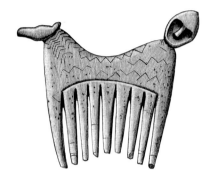

combs • Kämme • pettini • peignes • peines • pentes • ヘアピン • 梳子

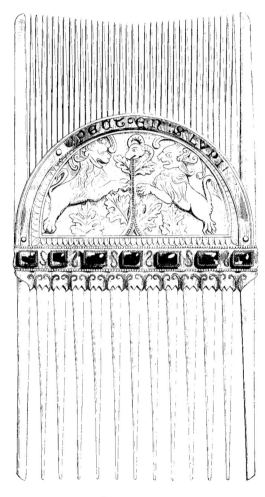

combs • Kämme • pettini • peignes • peines • pentes • ヘアピン • 梳子

hairpins • Haarnadeln • fermagli • épingles à cheveux • horquillas • ganchos • ヘアピン • 发夹

hairpins • Haarnadeln • fermagli • épingles à cheveux • horquillas • ganchos • ヘアピン • 发夹

hairpins • Haarnadeln • fermagli • épingles à cheveux • horquillas • ganchos • ヘアピン • 发夹

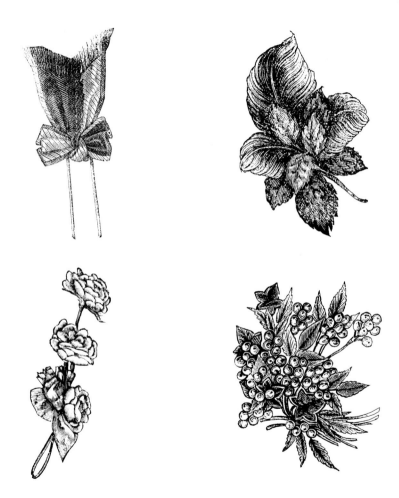

hairpins • Haarnadeln • fermagli • épingles à cheveux • horquillas • ganchos • ヘアピン • 发夹

hairpins • Haarnadeln • fermagli • épingles à cheveux • horquillas • ganchos • ヘアピン • 发夹

hairpins • Haarnadeln • fermagli • épingles à cheveux • horquillas • ganchos • ヘアピン • 发夹

hairpins • Haarnadeln • fermagli • épingles à cheveux • horquillas • ganchos • ヘアピン • 发夹

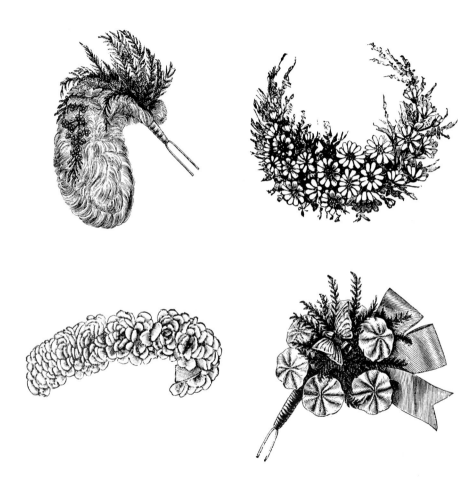

hairpins • Haarnadeln • fermagli • épingles à cheveux • horquillas • ganchos • ヘアピン • 发夹

hairpins • Haarnadeln • fermagli • épingles à cheveux • horquillas • ganchos • ヘアピン • 发夹

hairpins • Haarnadeln • fermagli • épingles à cheveux • horquillas • ganchos • ヘアピン • 发夹

hairpins • Haarnadeln • fermagli • épingles à cheveux • horquillas • ganchos • ヘアピン • 发夹

hairpins • Haarnadeln • fermagli • épingles à cheveux • horquillas • ganchos • ヘアピン • 发夹

hairpins • Haarnadeln • fermagli • épingles à cheveux • horquillas • ganchos • ヘアピン • 发夹

hairpins • Haarnadeln • fermagli • épingles à cheveux • horquillas • ganchos • ヘアピン • 发夹

spectacles • Brillen • occhiali • lunettes • anteojos • óculos • めがね • 眼镜

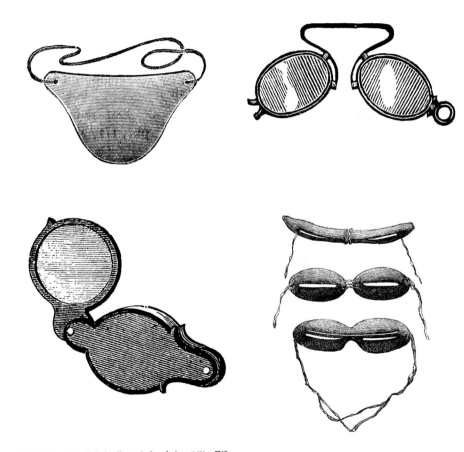

spectacles • Brillen • occhiali • lunettes • anteojos • óculos • めがね • 眼镜

nose decorations • Nasenschmuck • decorazioni per il naso • ornements pour le nez • adornos para la nariz • ornamentos para o nariz • 鼻飾り • 鼻饰

nose decorations • Nasenschmuck • decorazioni per il naso • ornements pour le nez • adornos para la nariz • ornamentos para o nariz • 鼻飾り • 鼻饰

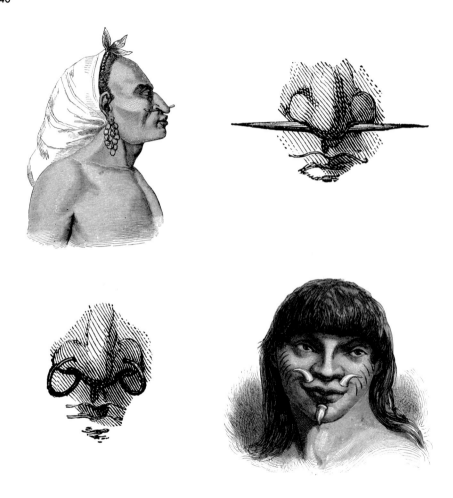

nose decorations • Nasenschmuck • decorazioni per il naso • ornements pour le nez • adornos para la nariz • ornamentos para o nariz • 鼻飾り • 鼻饰

nose decorations • Nasenschmuck • decorazioni per il naso • ornements pour le nez • adornos para la nariz • ornamentos para o nariz • 鼻飾り • 鼻饰

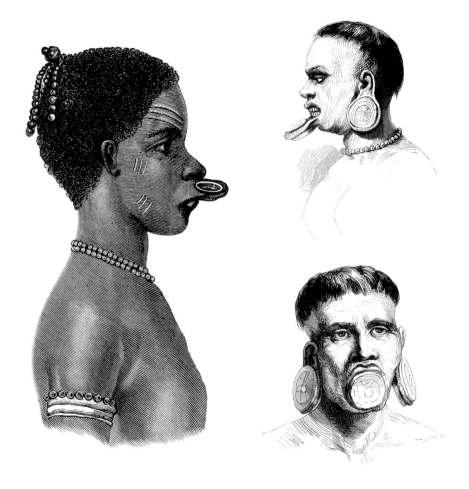

lip decorations • Lippenschmuck • decorazioni per le labbra • ornements pour les lèvres
adornos para los labios • Ornamentos para os lábios • 口飾り • 唇饰

143

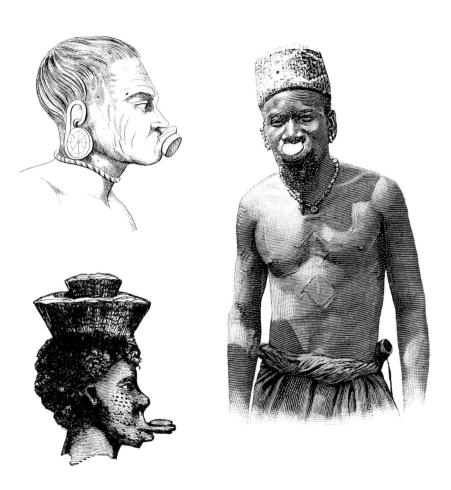

lip decorations • Lippenschmuck • decorazioni per le labbra • ornements pour les lèvres
adornos para los labios • Ornamentos para os lábios • 口飾り • 唇饰

earrings • Ohrringe • orecchini • boucles d'oreille • pendientes • brincos • イヤリング • 耳环

earrings • Ohrringe • orecchini • boucles d'oreille • pendientes • brincos • イヤリング • 耳环

earrings • Ohrringe • orecchini • boucles d'oreille • pendientes • brincos • イヤリング • 耳环

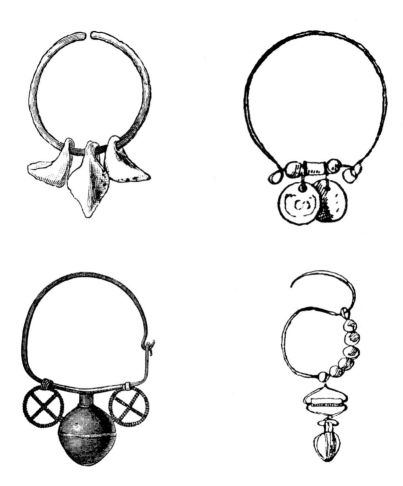

earrings • Ohrringe • orecchini • boucles d'oreille • pendientes • brincos • イヤリング • 耳环

earrings • Ohrringe • orecchini • boucles d'oreille • pendientes • brincos • イヤリング • 耳环

earrings • Ohrringe • orecchini • boucles d'oreille • pendientes • brincos • イヤリング • 耳环

earrings • Ohrringe • orecchini • boucles d'oreille • pendientes • brincos • イヤリング • 耳环

earrings • Ohrringe • orecchini • boucles d'oreille • pendientes • brincos • イヤリング • 耳环

earrings • Ohrringe • orecchini • boucles d'oreille • pendientes • brincos • イヤリング • 耳环

earrings • Ohrringe • orecchini • boucles d'oreille • pendientes • brincos • イヤリング • 耳环

necklaces and pendants • Halsketten und Anhänger • collane e ciondoli • colliers et pendentifs
collares y colgantes • fios e pendentes • ネックレスとペンダント • 项链和吊坠

necklaces and pendants • Halsketten und Anhänger • collane e ciondoli • colliers et pendentifs
collares y colgantes • fios e pendentes • ネックレスとペンダント • 项链和吊坠

necklaces and pendants • Halsketten und Anhänger • collane e ciondoli • colliers et pendentifs
collares y colgantes • fios e pendentes • ネックレスとペンダント • 项链和吊坠

necklaces and pendants • Halsketten und Anhänger • collane e ciondoli • colliers et pendentifs
collares y colgantes • fios e pendentes • ネックレスとペンダント • 项链和吊坠

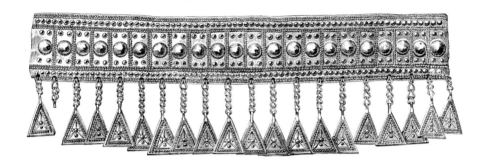

necklaces and pendants • Halsketten und Anhänger • collane e ciondoli • colliers et pendentifs
collares y colgantes • fios e pendentes • ネックレスとペンダント • 项链和吊坠

necklaces and pendants • Halsketten und Anhänger • collane e ciondoli • colliers et pendentifs
collares y colgantes • fios e pendentes • ネックレスとペンダント • 项链和吊坠

necklaces and pendants • Halsketten und Anhänger • collane e ciondoli • colliers et pendentifs
collares y colgantes • fios e pendentes • ネックレスとペンダント • 项链和吊坠

necklaces and pendants • Halsketten und Anhänger • collane e ciondoli • colliers et pendentifs
collares y colgantes • fios e pendentes • ネックレスとペンダント • 项链和吊坠

necklaces and pendants • Halsketten und Anhänger • collane e ciondoli • colliers et pendentifs
collares y colgantes • fios e pendentes • ネックレスとペンダント • 项链和吊坠

necklaces and pendants • Halsketten und Anhänger • collane e ciondoli • colliers et pendentifs
collares y colgantes • fios e pendentes • ネックレスとペンダント • 项链和吊坠

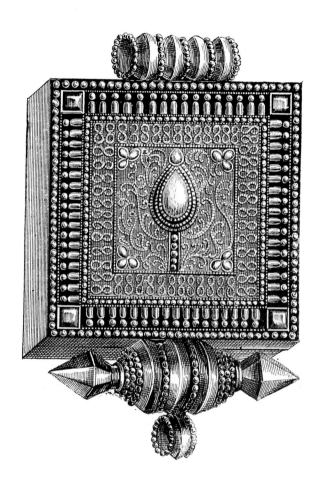

necklaces and pendants • Halsketten und Anhänger • collane e ciondoli • colliers et pendentifs
collares y colgantes • fios e pendentes • ネックレスとペンダント • 项链和吊坠

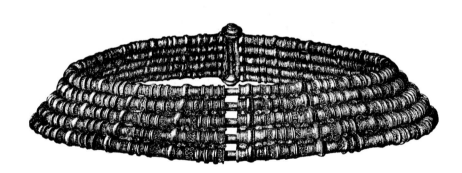

necklaces and pendants • Halsketten und Anhänger • collane e ciondoli • colliers et pendentifs
collares y colgantes • fios e pendentes • ネックレスとペンダント • 项链和吊坠

necklaces and pendants • Halsketten und Anhänger • collane e ciondoli • colliers et pendentifs
collares y colgantes • fios e pendentes • ネックレスとペンダント • 项链和吊坠

necklaces and pendants • Halsketten und Anhänger • collane e ciondoli • colliers et pendentifs
collares y colgantes • fios e pendentes • ネックレスとペンダント • 项链和吊坠

necklaces and pendants • Halsketten und Anhänger • collane e ciondoli • colliers et pendentifs
collares y colgantes • fios e pendentes • ネックレスとペンダント • 项链和吊坠

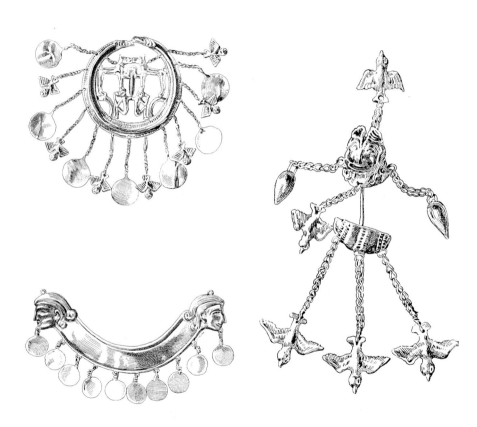

necklaces and pendants • Halsketten und Anhänger • collane e ciondoli • colliers et pendentifs
collares y colgantes • fios e pendentes • ネックレスとペンダント • 项链和吊坠

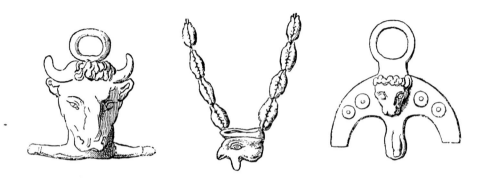

necklaces and pendants • Halsketten und Anhänger • collane e ciondoli • colliers et pendentifs
collares y colgantes • fios e pendentes • ネックレスとペンダント • 项链和吊坠

necklaces and pendants • Halsketten und Anhänger • collane e ciondoli • colliers et pendentifs
collares y colgantes • fios e pendentes • ネックレスとペンダント • 项链和吊坠

172

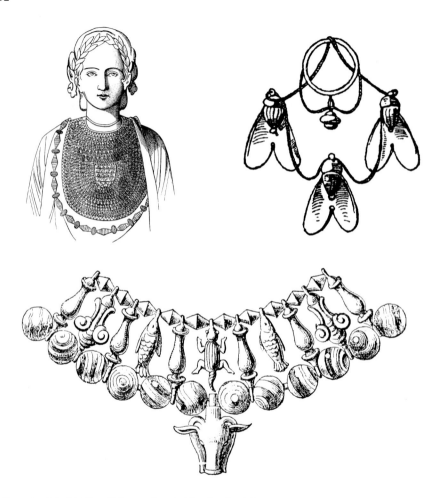

necklaces and pendants • Halsketten und Anhänger • collane e ciondoli • colliers et pendentifs
collares y colgantes • fios e pendentes • ネックレスとペンダント • 项链和吊坠

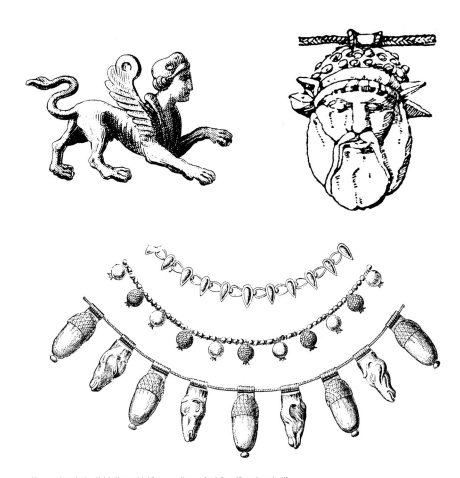

necklaces and pendants • Halsketten und Anhänger • collane e ciondoli • colliers et pendentifs
collares y colgantes • fios e pendentes • ネックレスとペンダント • 项链和吊坠

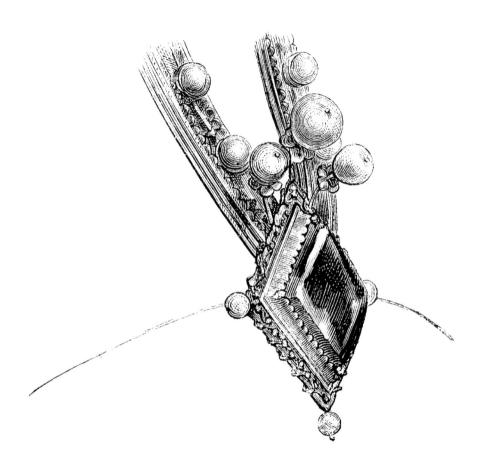

necklaces and pendants • Halsketten und Anhänger • collane e ciondoli • colliers et pendentifs
collares y colgantes • fios e pendentes • ネックレスとペンダント • 项链和吊坠

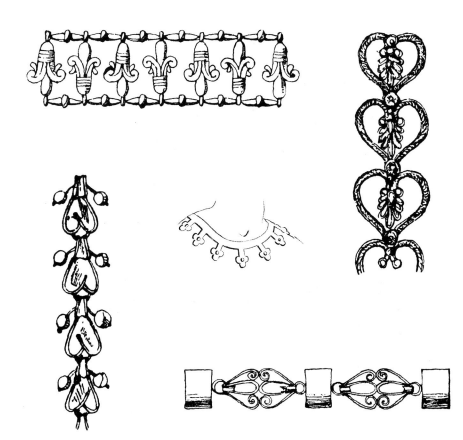

necklaces and pendants • Halsketten und Anhänger • collane e ciondoli • colliers et pendentifs
collares y colgantes • fios e pendentes • ネックレスとペンダント • 项链和吊坠

necklaces and pendants • Halsketten und Anhänger • collane e ciondoli • colliers et pendentifs
collares y colgantes • fios e pendentes • ネックレスとペンダント • 项链和吊坠

necklaces and pendants • Halsketten und Anhänger • collane e ciondoli • colliers et pendentifs
collares y colgantes • fios e pendentes • ネックレスとペンダント • 项链和吊坠

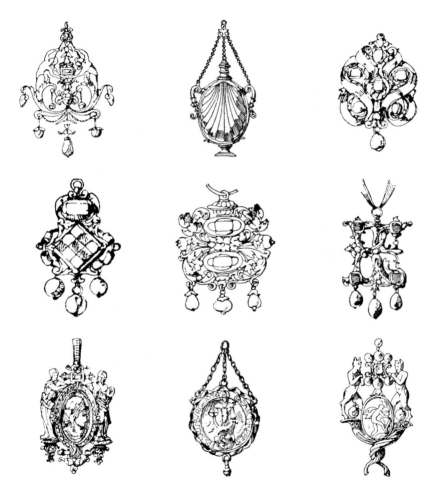

necklaces and pendants • Halsketten und Anhänger • collane e ciondoli • colliers et pendentifs
collares y colgantes • fios e pendentes • ネックレスとペンダント • 项链和吊坠

necklaces and pendants • Halsketten und Anhänger • collane e ciondoli • colliers et pendentifs
collares y colgantes • fios e pendentes • ネックレスとペンダント • 项链和吊坠

necklaces and pendants • Halsketten und Anhänger • collane e ciondoli • colliers et pendentifs
collares y colgantes • fios e pendentes • ネックレスとペンダント • 项链和吊坠

necklaces and pendants • Halsketten und Anhänger • collane e ciondoli • colliers et pendentifs
collares y colgantes • fios e pendentes • ネックレスとペンダント • 项链和吊坠

necklaces and pendants • Halsketten und Anhänger • collane e ciondoli • colliers et pendentifs
collares y colgantes • fios e pendentes • ネックレスとペンダント • 项链和吊坠

necklaces and pendants • Halsketten und Anhänger • collane e ciondoli • colliers et pendentifs
collares y colgantes • fios e pendentes • ネックレスとペンダント • 项链和吊坠

necklaces and pendants • Halsketten und Anhänger • collane e ciondoli • colliers et pendentifs
collares y colgantes • fios e pendentes • ネックレスとペンダント • 项链和吊坠

necklaces and pendants • Halsketten und Anhänger • collane e ciondoli • colliers et pendentifs
collares y colgantes • fios e pendentes • ネックレスとペンダント • 项链和吊坠

necklaces and pendants • Halsketten und Anhänger • collane e ciondoli • colliers et pendentifs
collares y colgantes • fios e pendentes • ネックレスとペンダント • 项链和吊坠

necklaces and pendants • Halsketten und Anhänger • collane e ciondoli • colliers et pendentifs
collares y colgantes • fios e pendentes • ネックレスとペンダント • 项链和吊坠

necklaces and pendants • Halsketten und Anhänger • collane e ciondoli • colliers et pendentifs
collares y colgantes • fios e pendentes • ネックレスとペンダント • 项链和吊坠

necklaces and pendants • Halsketten und Anhänger • collane e ciondoli • colliers et pendentifs
collares y colgantes • fios e pendentes • ネックレスとペンダント • 项链和吊坠

necklaces and pendants • Halsketten und Anhänger • collane e ciondoli • colliers et pendentifs
collares y colgantes • fios e pendentes • ネックレスとペンダント • 项链和吊坠

necklaces and pendants • Halsketten und Anhänger • collane e ciondoli • colliers et pendentifs
collares y colgantes • fios e pendentes • ネックレスとペンダント • 项链和吊坠

necklaces and pendants • Halsketten und Anhänger • collane e ciondoli • colliers et pendentifs
collares y colgantes • fios e pendentes • ネックレスとペンダント • 项链和吊坠

necklaces and pendants • Halsketten und Anhänger • collane e ciondoli • colliers et pendentifs
collares y colgantes • fios e pendentes • ネックレスとペンダント • 项链和吊坠

collars • Kragen • collari • cols • cuellos • colares • 襟飾り • 项饰

collars • Kragen • collari • cols • cuellos • colares • 襟飾り • 项饰

collars • Kragen • collari • cols • cuellos • colares • 襟飾り • 项饰

collars • Kragen • collari • cols • cuellos • colares • 襟飾り • 项饰

collars • Kragen • collari • cols • cuellos • colares • 襟飾り • 项饰

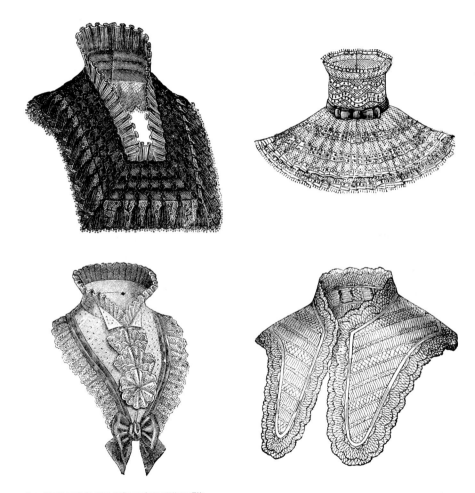

collars • Kragen • collari • cols • cuellos • colares • 襟飾り • 项饰

collars • Kragen • collari • cols • cuellos • colares • 襟飾り • 项饰

ties and scarves • Krawatten und Schals • cravatte e foulard • cravates et écharpes
corbatas y bufandas • gravatas e lenços • ネクタイとスカーフ • 领带和围巾

ties and scarves • Krawatten und Schals • cravatte e foulard • cravates et écharpes
corbatas y bufandas • gravatas e lenços • ネクタイとスカーフ • 领带和围巾

ties and scarves • Krawatten und Schals • cravatte e foulard • cravates et écharpes
corbatas y bufandas • gravatas e lenços • ネクタイとスカーフ • 领带和围巾

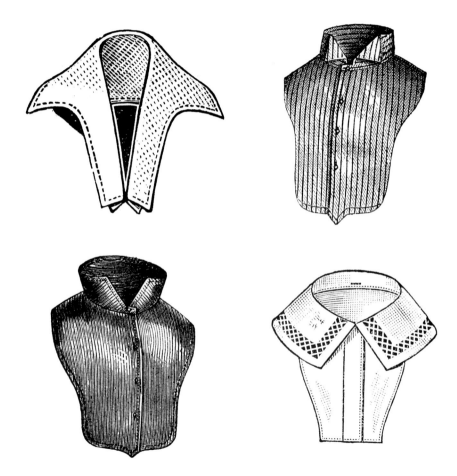

collars • Kragen • collari • cols • cuellos • colares • 襟飾り • 项饰

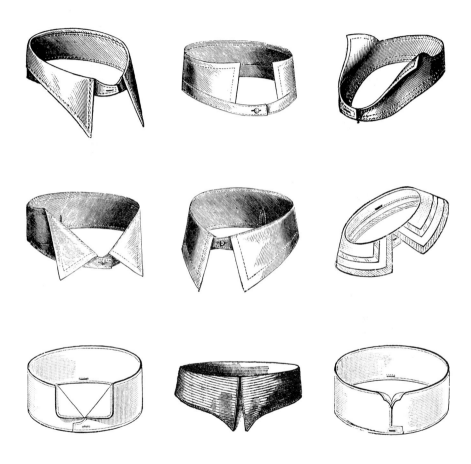

collars • Kragen • collari • cols • cuellos • colares • 襟飾り • 项饰

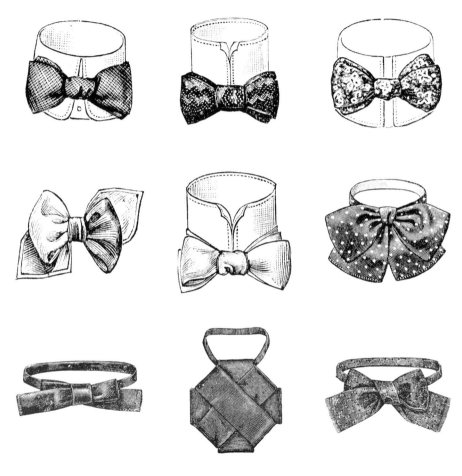

ties and scarves • Krawatten und Schals • cravatte e foulard • cravates et écharpes
corbatas y bufandas • gravatas e lenços • ネクタイとスカーフ • 领带和围巾

ties and scarves • Krawatten und Schals • cravatte e foulard • cravates et écharpes
corbatas y bufandas • gravatas e lenços • ネクタイとスカーフ • 领带和围巾

ties and scarves • Krawatten und Schals • cravatte e foulard • cravates et écharpes
corbatas y bufandas • gravatas e lenços • ネクタイとスカーフ • 领带和围巾

ties and scarves • Krawatten und Schals • cravatte e foulard • cravates et écharpes
corbatas y bufandas • gravatas e lenços • ネクタイとスカーフ • 领带和围巾

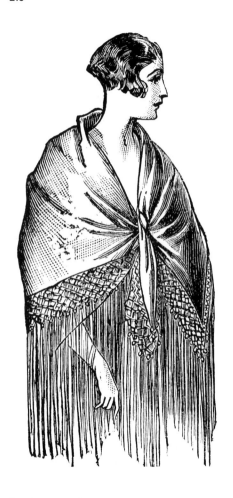

ties and scarves • Krawatten und Schals • cravatte e foulard • cravates et écharpes
corbatas y bufandas • gravatas e lenços • ネクタイとスカーフ • 领带和围巾

ties and scarves • Krawatten und Schals • cravatte e foulard • cravates et écharpes
corbatas y bufandas • gravatas e lenços • ネクタイとスカーフ • 领带和围巾

fibulae, pins and brooches • Fibeln, Anstecknadeln und Broschen • fibula, spille e brooche • fermoirs, épingles et broches
fíbulas, alfileres y broches • fíbulas, alfinetes e broches • 留め針、ピン、ブローチ • 胸针、别针和胸花

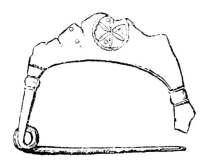

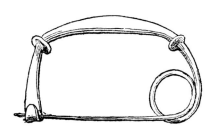

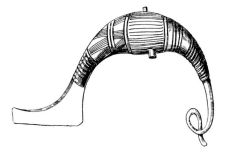

fibulae, pins and brooches • Fibeln, Anstecknadeln und Broschen • fibula, spille e brooche • fermoirs, épingles et broches
fíbulas, alfileres y broches • fíbulas, alfinetes e broches • 留め針、ピン、ブローチ • 胸针、别针和胸花

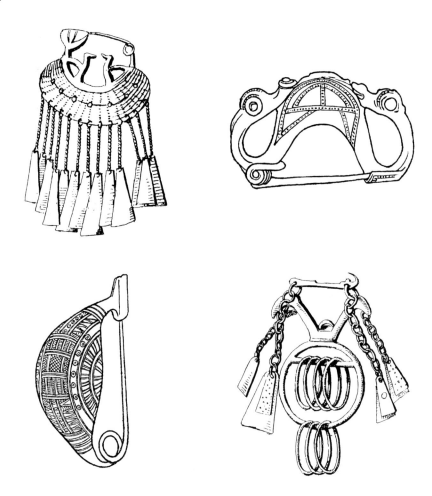

fibulae, pins and brooches • Fibeln, Anstecknadeln und Broschen • fibula, spille e brooche • fermoirs, épingles et broches
fíbulas, alfileres y broches • fíbulas, alfinetes e broches • 留め針、ピン、ブローチ • 胸针、别针和胸花

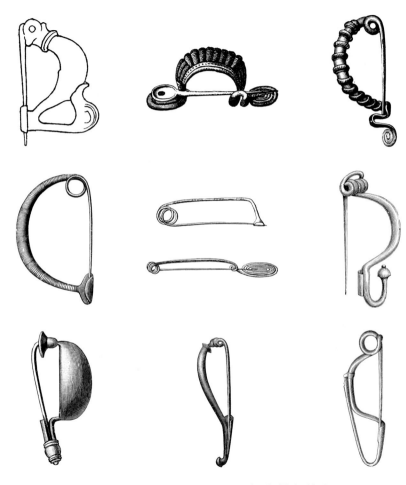

fibulae, pins and brooches • Fibeln, Anstecknadeln und Broschen • fibula, spille e brooche • fermoirs, épingles et broches
fíbulas, alfileres y broches • fíbulas, alfinetes e broches • 留め針、ピン、ブローチ • 胸针、别针和胸花

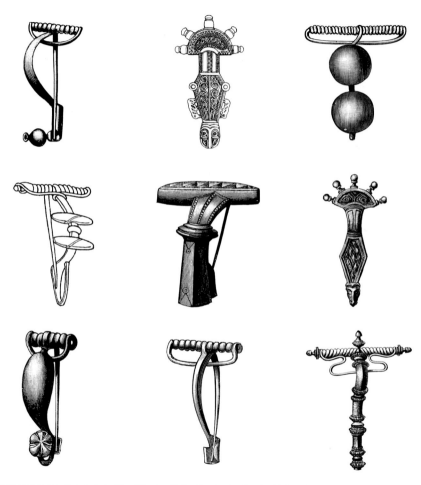

fibulae, pins and brooches • Fibeln, Anstecknadeln und Broschen • fibula, spille e brooche • fermoirs, épingles et broches
fíbulas, alfileres y broches • fíbulas, alfinetes e broches • 留め針、ピン、ブローチ • 胸针、别针和胸花

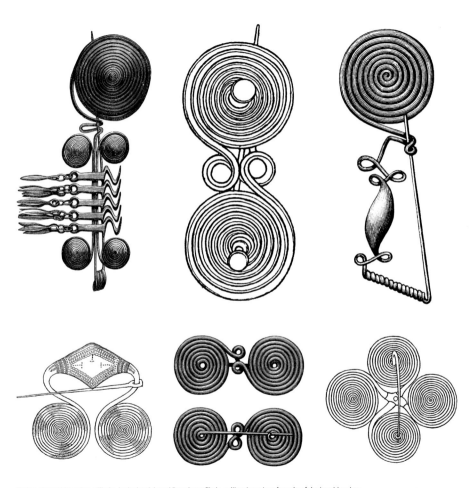

fibulae, pins and brooches • Fibeln, Anstecknadeln und Broschen • fibula, spille e brooche • fermoirs, épingles et broches
fíbulas, alfileres y broches • fíbulas, alfinetes e broches • 留め針、ピン、ブローチ • 胸针、别针和胸花

fibulae, pins and brooches • Fibeln, Anstecknadeln und Broschen • fibula, spille e brooche • fermoirs, épingles et broches
fíbulas, alfileres y broches • fíbulas, alfinetes e broches • 留め針、ピン、ブローチ • 胸针、别针和胸花

fibulae, pins and brooches • Fibeln, Anstecknadeln und Broschen • fibula, spille e brooche • fermoirs, épingles et broches
fíbulas, alfileres y broches • fíbulas, alfinetes e broches • 留め針、ピン、ブローチ • 胸针、别针和胸花

fibulae, pins and brooches • Fibeln, Anstecknadeln und Broschen • fibula, spille e brooche • fermoirs, épingles et broches
fíbulas, alfileres y broches • fíbulas, alfinetes e broches • 留め針、ピン、ブローチ • 胸针、别针和胸花

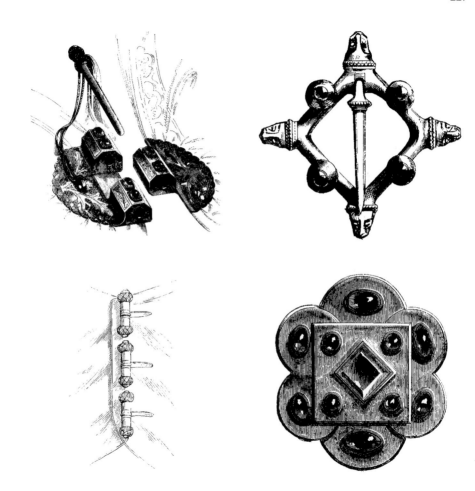

fibulae, pins and brooches • Fibeln, Anstecknadeln und Broschen • fibula, spille e brooche • fermoirs, épingles et broches
fíbulas, alfileres y broches • fíbulas, alfinetes e broches • 留め針、ピン、ブローチ • 胸针、别针和胸花

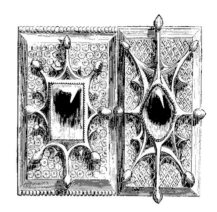

fibulae, pins and brooches • Fibeln, Anstecknadeln und Broschen • fibula, spille e brooche • fermoirs, épingles et broches
fíbulas, alfileres y broches • fíbulas, alfinetes e broches • 留め針、ピン、ブローチ • 胸针、别针和胸花

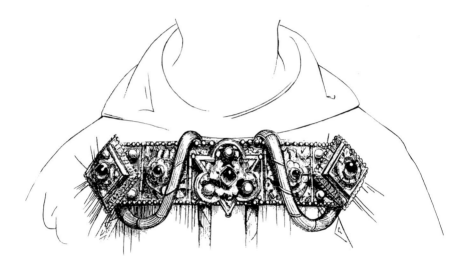

fibulae, pins and brooches • Fibeln, Anstecknadeln und Broschen • fibula, spille e brooche • fermoirs, épingles et broches
fíbulas, alfileres y broches • fíbulas, alfinetes e broches • 留め針、ピン、ブローチ • 胸针、别针和胸花

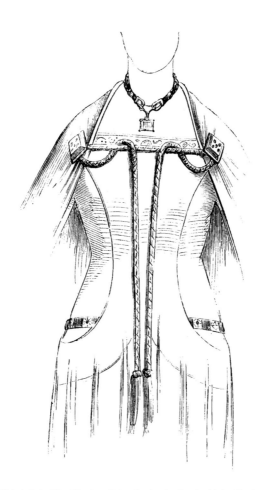

fibulae, pins and brooches • Fibeln, Anstecknadeln und Broschen • fibula, spille e brooche • fermoirs, épingles et broches
fíbulas, alfileres y broches • fíbulas, alfinetes e broches • 留め針、ピン、ブローチ • 胸针、别针和胸花

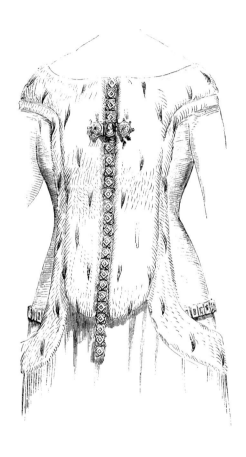

fibulae, pins and brooches • Fibeln, Anstecknadeln und Broschen • fibula, spille e brooche • fermoirs, épingles et broches
fíbulas, alfileres y broches • fíbulas, alfinetes e broches • 留め針、ピン、ブローチ • 胸针、别针和胸花

fibulae, pins and brooches • Fibeln, Anstecknadeln und Broschen • fibula, spille e brooche • fermoirs, épingles et broches
fíbulas, alfileres y broches • fíbulas, alfinetes e broches • 留め針、ピン、ブローチ • 胸针、别针和胸花

fibulae, pins and brooches • Fibeln, Anstecknadeln und Broschen • fibula, spille e brooche • fermoirs, épingles et broches
fíbulas, alfileres y broches • fíbulas, alfinetes e broches • 留め針、ピン、ブローチ • 胸针、别针和胸花

fibulae, pins and brooches • Fibeln, Anstecknadeln und Broschen • fibula, spille e brooche • fermoirs, épingles et broches
fíbulas, alfileres y broches • fíbulas, alfinetes e broches • 留め針、ピン、ブローチ • 胸针、别针和胸花

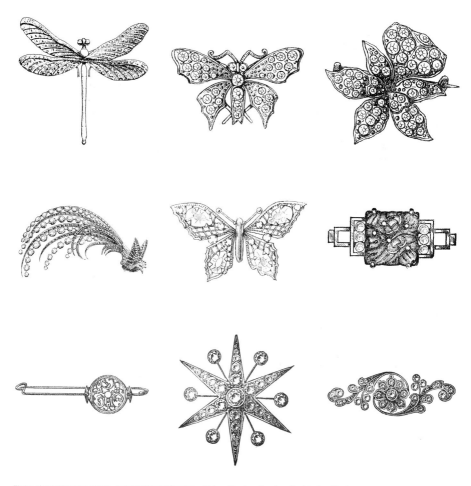

fibulae, pins and brooches • Fibeln, Anstecknadeln und Broschen • fibula, spille e brooche • fermoirs, épingles et broches
fíbulas, alfileres y broches • fíbulas, alfinetes e broches • 留め針、ピン、ブローチ • 胸针、别针和胸花

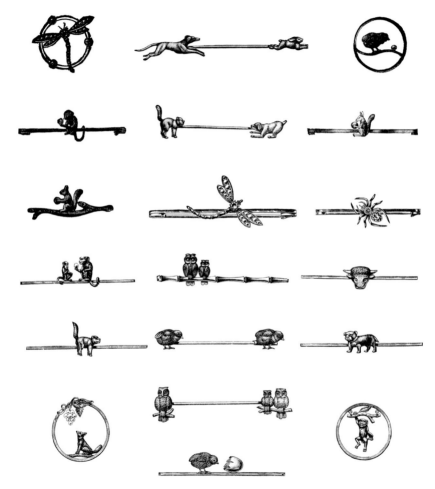

fibulae, pins and brooches • Fibeln, Anstecknadeln und Broschen • fibula, spille e brooche • fermoirs, épingles et broches
fíbulas, alfileres y broches • fíbulas, alfinetes e broches • 留め針、ピン、ブローチ • 胸针、别针和胸花

fibulae, pins and brooches • Fibeln, Anstecknadeln und Broschen • fibula, spille e brooche • fermoirs, épingles et broches
fíbulas, alfileres y broches • fíbulas, alfinetes e broches • 留め針、ピン、ブローチ • 胸针、别针和胸花

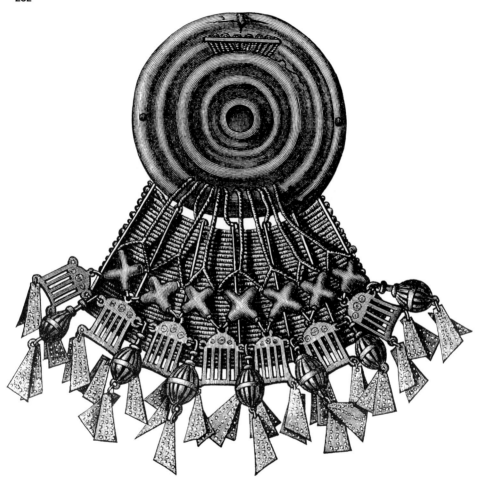

fibulae, pins and brooches • Fibeln, Anstecknadeln und Broschen • fibula, spille e brooche • fermoirs, épingles et broches
fíbulas, alfileres y broches • fíbulas, alfinetes e broches • 留め針、ピン、ブローチ • 胸针、别针和胸花

fibulae, pins and brooches • Fibeln, Anstecknadeln und Broschen • fibula, spille e brooche • fermoirs, épingles et broches
fíbulas, alfileres y broches • fíbulas, alfinetes e broches • 留め針、ピン、ブローチ • 胸针、别针和胸花

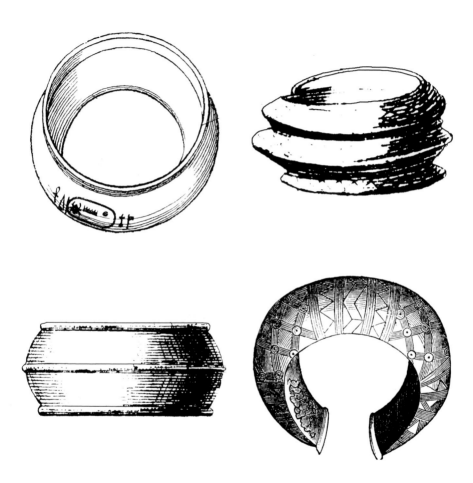

bracelets and wrist decorations • Armbänder und Armschmuck • braccialetti e decorazioni per il braccio • ornements pour bras et poignets
pulseras y adornos para los brazos • braceletes e ornamentos para o braço • 腕飾りとブレスレット • 臂饰和腕饰

bracelets and wrist decorations • Armbänder und Armschmuck • braccialetti e decorazioni per il braccio • ornements pour bras et poignets
pulseras y adornos para los brazos • braceletes e ornamentos para o braço • 腕飾りとブレスレット • 臂饰和腕饰

bracelets and wrist decorations • Armbänder und Armschmuck • braccialetti e decorazioni per il braccio • ornements pour bras et poignets
pulseras y adornos para los brazos • braceletes e ornamentos para o braço • 腕飾りとブレスレット • 臂饰和腕饰

bracelets and wrist decorations • Armbänder und Armschmuck • braccialetti e decorazioni per il braccio • ornements pour bras et poignets
pulseras y adornos para los brazos • braceletes e ornamentos para o braço • 腕飾りとブレスレット • 臂饰和腕饰

bracelets and wrist decorations • Armbänder und Armschmuck • braccialetti e decorazioni per il braccio • ornements pour bras et poignets
pulseras y adornos para los brazos • braceletes e ornamentos para o braço • 腕飾りとブレスレット • 臂饰和腕饰

bracelets and wrist decorations • Armbänder und Armschmuck • braccialetti e decorazioni per il braccio • ornements pour bras et poignets
pulseras y adornos para los brazos • braceletes e ornamentos para o braço • 腕飾りとブレスレット • 臂饰和腕饰

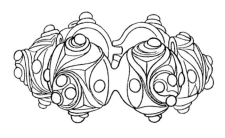
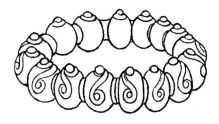
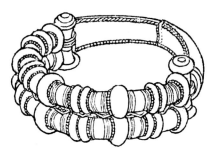

bracelets and wrist decorations • Armbänder und Armschmuck • braccialetti e decorazioni per il braccio • ornements pour bras et poignets
pulseras y adornos para los brazos • braceletes e ornamentos para o braço • 腕飾りとブレスレット • 臂饰和腕饰

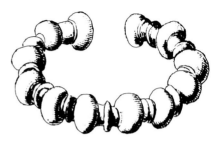
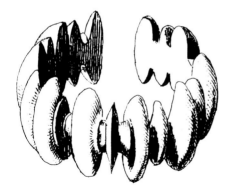

bracelets and wrist decorations • Armbänder und Armschmuck • braccialetti e decorazioni per il braccio • ornements pour bras et poignets
pulseras y adornos para los brazos • braceletes e ornamentos para o braço • 腕飾りとブレスレット • 臂饰和腕饰

bracelets and wrist decorations • Armbänder und Armschmuck • braccialetti e decorazioni per il braccio • ornements pour bras et poignets
pulseras y adornos para los brazos • braceletes e ornamentos para o braço • 腕飾りとブレスレット • 臂饰和腕饰

bracelets and wrist decorations • Armbänder und Armschmuck • braccialetti e decorazioni per il braccio • ornements pour bras et poignets
pulseras y adornos para los brazos • braceletes e ornamentos para o braço • 腕飾りとブレスレット • 臂饰和腕饰

bracelets and wrist decorations • Armbänder und Armschmuck • braccialetti e decorazioni per il braccio • ornements pour bras et poignets
pulseras y adornos para los brazos • braceletes e ornamentos para o braço • 腕飾りとブレスレット • 臂饰和腕饰

bracelets and wrist decorations • Armbänder und Armschmuck • braccialetti e decorazioni per il braccio • ornements pour bras et poignets
pulseras y adornos para los brazos • braceletes e ornamentos para o braço • 腕飾りとブレスレット • 臂饰和腕饰

bracelets and wrist decorations • Armbänder und Armschmuck • braccialetti e decorazioni per il braccio • ornements pour bras et poignets
pulseras y adornos para los brazos • braceletes e ornamentos para o braço • 腕飾りとブレスレット • 臂饰和腕饰

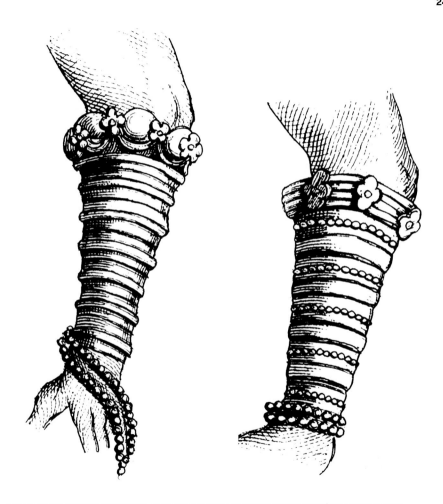

bracelets and wrist decorations • Armbänder und Armschmuck • braccialetti e decorazioni per il braccio • ornements pour bras et poignets
pulseras y adornos para los brazos • braceletes e ornamentos para o braço • 腕飾りとブレスレット • 臂饰和腕饰

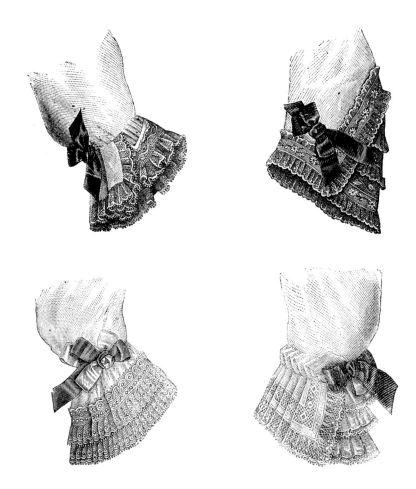

cuffs • Manschetten • polsi • manchettes • puños de camisa • punhos • カフス • 护腕

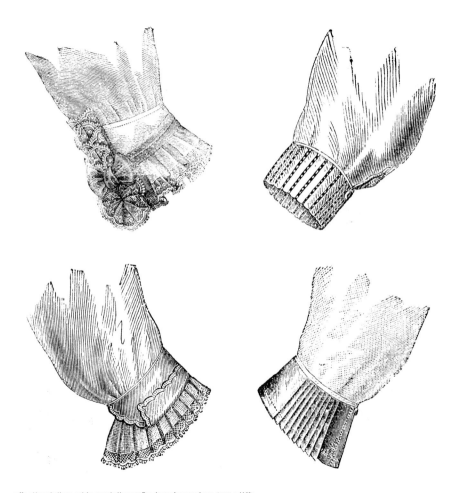

cuffs • Manschetten • polsi • manchettes • puños de camisa • punhos • カフス • 护腕

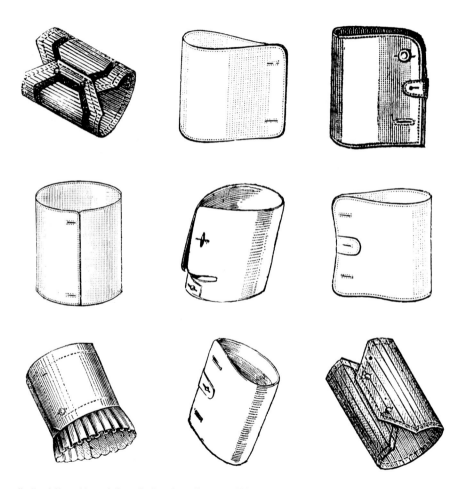

cuffs • Manschetten • polsi • manchettes • puños de camisa • punhos • カフス • 护腕

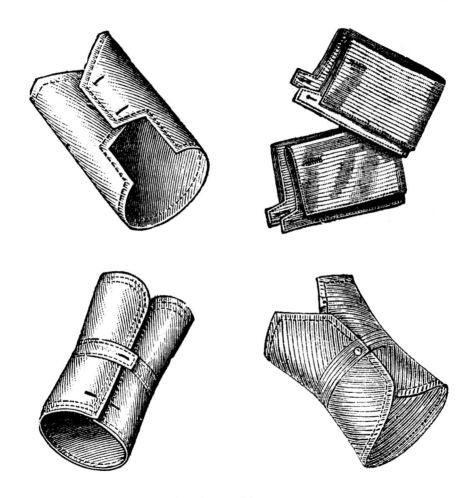

cuffs • Manschetten • polsi • manchettes • puños de camisa • punhos • カフス • 护腕

watches • Uhren • orologi • montres • relojes • relógios • 腕時計 • 手表

watches • Uhren • orologi • montres • relojes • relógios • 腕時計 • 手表

rings • Ringe • anelli • bagues • anillos • anéis • 指輪 • 戒指

rings • Ringe • anelli • bagues • anillos • anéis • 指輪 • 戒指

rings • Ringe • anelli • bagues • anillos • anéis • 指輪 • 戒指

rings • Ringe • anelli • bagues • anillos • anéis • 指輪 • 戒指

umbrellas • Schirme • ombrelli • parapluies • paraguas • chapéus-de-chuva • 傘 • 伞

umbrellas • Schirme • ombrelli • parapluies • paraguas • chapéus-de-chuva • 傘 • 傘

umbrellas • Schirme • ombrelli • parapluies • paraguas • chapéus-de-chuva • 傘 • 伞

umbrellas • Schirme • ombrelli • parapluies • paraguas • chapéus-de-chuva • 傘 • 傘

umbrellas • Schirme • ombrelli • parapluies • paraguas • chapéus-de-chuva • 傘 • 伞

umbrellas • Schirme • ombrelli • parapluies • paraguas • chapéus-de-chuva • 傘 • 伞

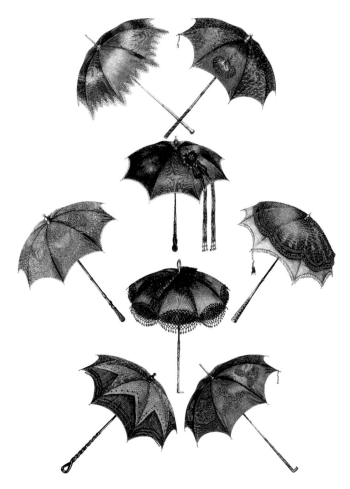

umbrellas • Schirme • ombrelli • parapluies • paraguas • chapéus-de-chuva • 傘 • 伞

umbrellas • Schirme • ombrelli • parapluies • paraguas • chapéus-de-chuva • 傘 • 伞

umbrellas • Schirme • ombrelli • parapluies • paraguas • chapéus-de-chuva • 傘 • 傘

umbrellas • Schirme • ombrelli • parapluies • paraguas • chapéus-de-chuva • 傘 • 伞

fans • Fächer • ventagli • éventails • abanicos • leques • 扇子 • 扇子

fans • Fächer • ventagli • éventails • abanicos • leques • 扇子 • 扇子

fans • Fächer • ventagli • éventails • abanicos • leques • 扇子 • 扇子

fans • Fächer • ventagli • éventails • abanicos • leques • 扇子 • 扇子

fans • Fächer • ventagli • éventails • abanicos • leques • 扇子 • 扇子

fans • Fächer • ventagli • éventails • abanicos • leques • 扇子 • 扇子

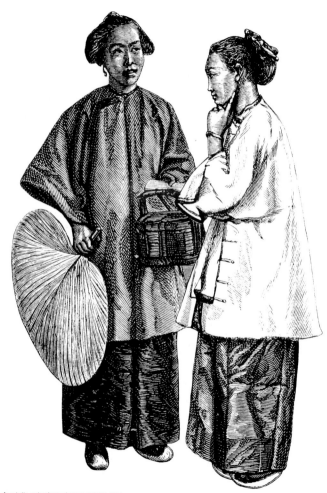

fans • Fächer • ventagli • éventails • abanicos • leques • 扇子 • 扇子

fans • Fächer • ventagli • éventails • abanicos • leques • 扇子 • 扇子

fans • Fächer • ventagli • éventails • abanicos • leques • 扇子 • 扇子

fans • Fächer • ventagli • éventails • abanicos • leques • 扇子 • 扇子

fans • Fächer • ventagli • éventails • abanicos • leques • 扇子 • 扇子

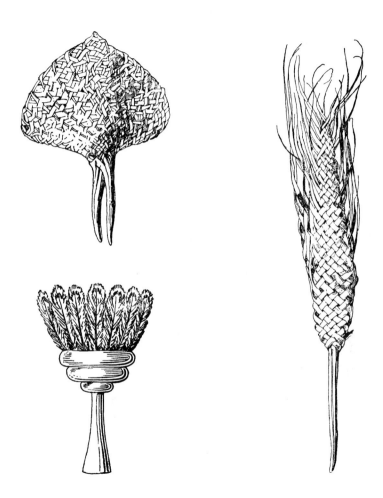

fans • Fächer • ventagli • éventails • abanicos • leques • 扇子 • 扇子

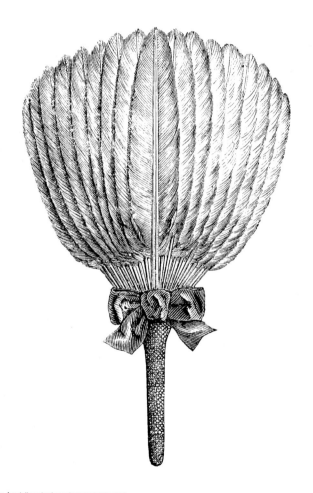

fans • Fächer • ventagli • éventails • abanicos • leques • 扇子 • 扇子

fans • Fächer • ventagli • éventails • abanicos • leques • 扇子 • 扇子

fans • Fächer • ventagli • éventails • abanicos • leques • 扇子 • 扇子

fans • Fächer • ventagli • éventails • abanicos • leques • 扇子 • 扇子

fans • Fächer • ventagli • éventails • abanicos • leques • 扇子 • 扇子

fans • Fächer • ventagli • éventails • abanicos • leques • 扇子 • 扇子

bags and purses • Taschen und Geldbörsen • sacche e borse • sacs et porte-monnaie
bolsos y monederos • malas e bolsas • バッグと財布 • 包和钱包

bags and purses • Taschen und Geldbörsen • sacche e borse • sacs et porte-monnaie
bolsos y monederos • malas e bolsas • バッグと財布 • 包和钱包

bags and purses • Taschen und Geldbörsen • sacche e borse • sacs et porte-monnaie
bolsos y monederos • malas e bolsas • バッグと財布 • 包和钱包

bags and purses • Taschen und Geldbörsen • sacche e borse • sacs et porte-monnaie
bolsos y monederos • malas e bolsas • バッグと財布 • 包和钱包

bags and purses • Taschen und Geldbörsen • sacche e borse • sacs et porte-monnaie
bolsos y monederos • malas e bolsas • バッグと財布 • 包和钱包

bags and purses • Taschen und Geldbörsen • sacche e borse • sacs et porte-monnaie
bolsos y monederos • malas e bolsas • バッグと財布 • 包和钱包

292

bags and purses • Taschen und Geldbörsen • sacche e borse • sacs et porte-monnaie
bolsos y monederos • malas e bolsas • バッグと財布 • 包和钱包

bags and purses • Taschen und Geldbörsen • sacche e borse • sacs et porte-monnaie
bolsos y monederos • malas e bolsas • バッグと財布 • 包和钱包

bags and purses • Taschen und Geldbörsen • sacche e borse • sacs et porte-monnaie
bolsos y monederos • malas e bolsas • バッグと財布 • 包和钱包

bags and purses • Taschen und Geldbörsen • sacche e borse • sacs et porte-monnaie
bolsos y monederos • malas e bolsas • バッグと財布 • 包和钱包

bags and purses • Taschen und Geldbörsen • sacche e borse • sacs et porte-monnaie
bolsos y monederos • malas e bolsas • バッグと財布 • 包和钱包

bags and purses • Taschen und Geldbörsen • sacche e borse • sacs et porte-monnaie
bolsos y monederos • malas e bolsas • バッグと財布 • 包和钱包

bags and purses • Taschen und Geldbörsen • sacche e borse • sacs et porte-monnaie
bolsos y monederos • malas e bolsas • バッグと財布 • 包和钱包

bags and purses • Taschen und Geldbörsen • sacche e borse • sacs et porte-monnaie
bolsos y monederos • malas e bolsas • バッグと財布 • 包和钱包

bags and purses • Taschen und Geldbörsen • sacche e borse • sacs et porte-monnaie
bolsos y monederos • malas e bolsas • バッグと財布 • 包和钱包

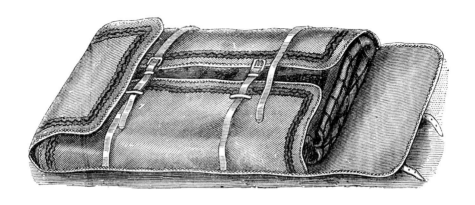

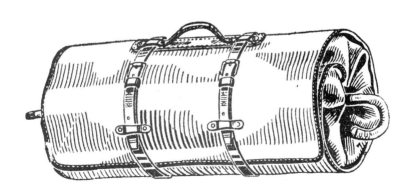

bags and purses • Taschen und Geldbörsen • sacche e borse • sacs et porte-monnaie
bolsos y monederos • malas e bolsas • バッグと財布 • 包和钱包

bags and purses • Taschen und Geldbörsen • sacche e borse • sacs et porte-monnaie
bolsos y monederos • malas e bolsas • バッグと財布 • 包和钱包

bags and purses • Taschen und Geldbörsen • sacche e borse • sacs et porte-monnaie
bolsos y monederos • malas e bolsas • バッグと財布 • 包和钱包

muffs and gloves • Muffe und Handschuhe • muffole e guanti • manchons et gants

manguitos y guantes • regalos e luvas • マフと手袋 • 手笼和手套

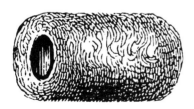

muffs and gloves • Muffe und Handschuhe • muffole e guanti • manchons et gants
manguitos y guantes • regalos e luvas • マフと手袋 • 手笼和手套

muffs and gloves • Muffe und Handschuhe • muffole e guanti • manchons et gants
manguitos y guantes • regalos e luvas • マフと手袋 • 手笼和手套

muffs and gloves • Muffe und Handschuhe • muffole e guanti • manchons et gants
manguitos y guantes • regalos e luvas • マフと手袋 • 手笼和手套

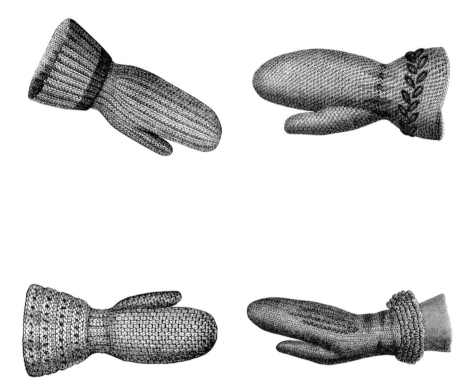

muffs and gloves • Muffe und Handschuhe • muffole e guanti • manchons et gants
manguitos y guantes • regalos e luvas • マフと手袋 • 手笼和手套

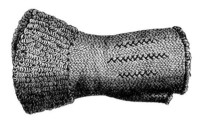

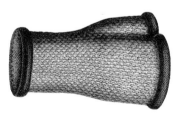

muffs and gloves • Muffe und Handschuhe • muffole e guanti • manchons et gants
manguitos y guantes • regalos e luvas • マフと手袋 • 手笼和手套

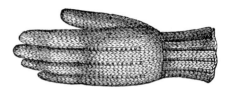

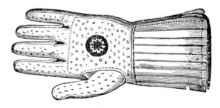

muffs and gloves • Muffe und Handschuhe • muffole e guanti • manchons et gants
manguitos y guantes • regalos e luvas • マフと手袋 • 手笼和手套

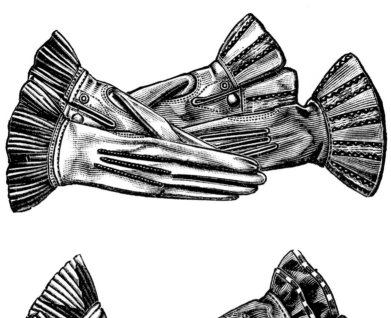

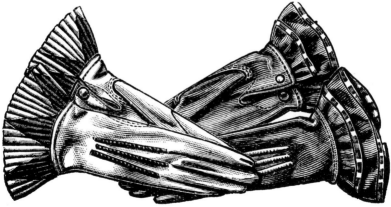

muffs and gloves • Muffe und Handschuhe • muffole e guanti • manchons et gants
manguitos y guantes • regalos e luvas • マフと手袋 • 手笼和手套

muffs and gloves • Muffe und Handschuhe • muffole e guanti • manchons et gants
manguitos y guantes • regalos e luvas • マフと手袋 • 手笼和手套

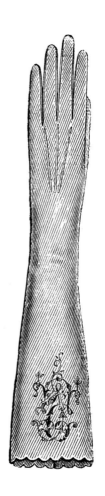

muffs and gloves • Muffe und Handschuhe • muffole e guanti • manchons et gants
manguitos y guantes • regalos e luvas • マフと手袋 • 手笼和手套

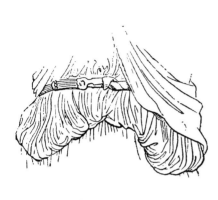

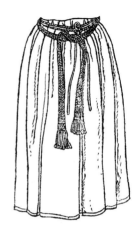

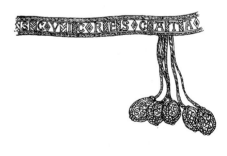

waistbands, belts and buckles • Taillenbänder, Gürtel und Schnallen • polsini, cinture e fibbie • ceintures et boucles de ceinture
pretinas, cinturones y hebillas • faixas, cintos e fivelas • ウエストバンド、ベルト、バックル • 腰带、皮带和搭扣

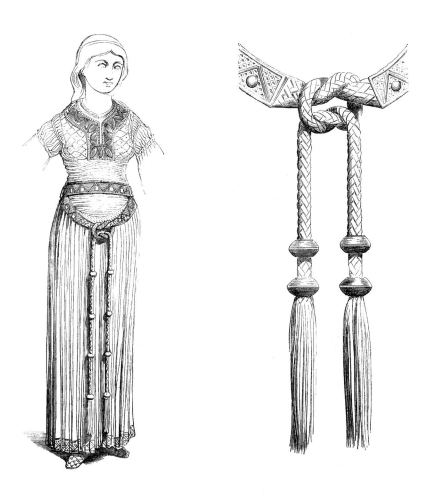

waistbands, belts and buckles • Taillenbänder, Gürtel und Schnallen • polsini, cinture e fibbie • ceintures et boucles de ceinture
pretinas, cinturones y hebillas • faixas, cintos e fivelas • ウエストバンド、ベルト、バックル • 腰带、皮带和搭扣

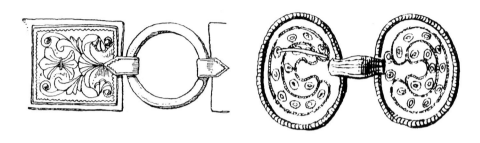

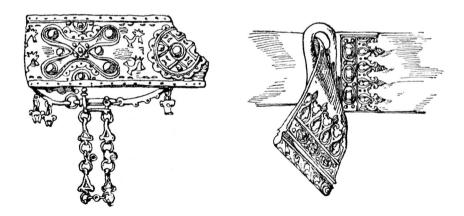

waistbands, belts and buckles • Taillenbänder, Gürtel und Schnallen • polsini, cinture e fibbie • ceintures et boucles de ceinture
pretinas, cinturones y hebillas • faixas, cintos e fivelas • ウエストバンド、ベルト、バックル • 腰带、皮带和搭扣

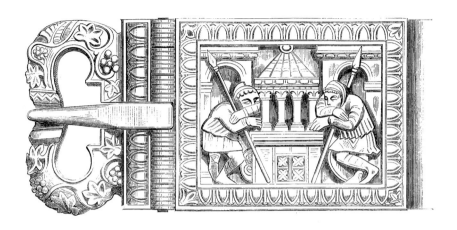

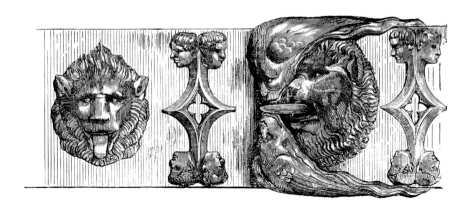

waistbands, belts and buckles • Taillenbänder, Gürtel und Schnallen • polsini, cinture e fibbie • ceintures et boucles de ceinture
pretinas, cinturones y hebillas • faixas, cintos e fivelas • ウエストバンド、ベルト、バックル • 腰带、皮帯和搭扣

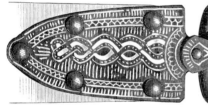

waistbands, belts and buckles • Taillenbänder, Gürtel und Schnallen • polsini, cinture e fibbie • ceintures et boucles de ceinture
pretinas, cinturones y hebillas • faixas, cintos e fivelas • ウエストバンド、ベルト、バックル • 腰带、皮带和搭扣

waistbands, belts and buckles • Taillenbänder, Gürtel und Schnallen • polsini, cinture e fibbie • ceintures et boucles de ceinture
pretinas, cinturones y hebillas • faixas, cintos e fivelas • ウエストバンド、ベルト、バックル • 腰带、皮带和搭扣

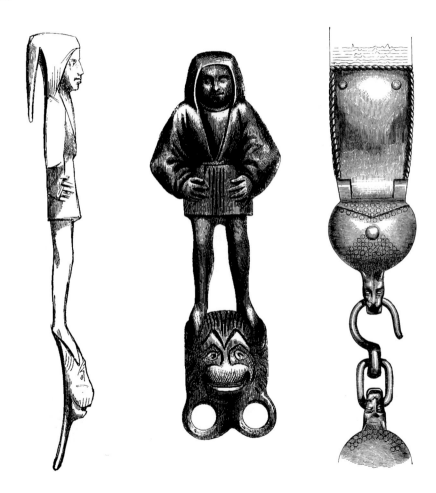

waistbands, belts and buckles • Taillenbänder, Gürtel und Schnallen • polsini, cinture e fibbie • ceintures et boucles de ceinture
pretinas, cinturones y hebillas • faixas, cintos e fivelas • ウエストバンド、ベルト、バックル • 腰带、皮带和搭扣

waistbands, belts and buckles • Taillenbänder, Gürtel und Schnallen • polsini, cinture e fibbie • ceintures et boucles de ceinture
pretinas, cinturones y hebillas • faixas, cintos e fivelas • ウエストバンド、ベルト、バックル • 腰带、皮带和搭扣

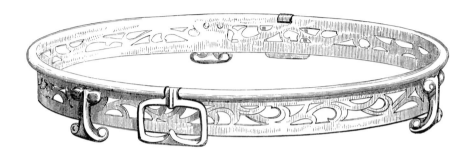

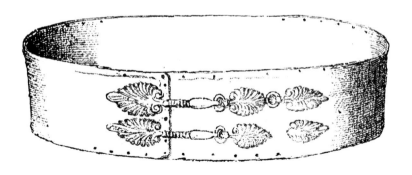

waistbands, belts and buckles • Taillenbänder, Gürtel und Schnallen • polsini, cinture e fibbie • ceintures et boucles de ceinture
pretinas, cinturones y hebillas • faixas, cintos e fivelas • ウエストバンド、ベルト、バックル • 腰带、皮带和搭扣

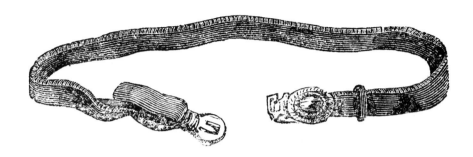

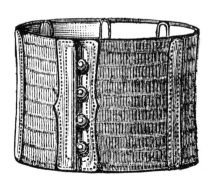

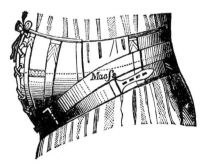

waistbands, belts and buckles • Taillenbänder, Gürtel und Schnallen • polsini, cinture e fibbie • ceintures et boucles de ceinture
pretinas, cinturones y hebillas • faixas, cintos e fivelas • ウエストバンド、ベルト、バックル • 腰带、皮带和搭扣

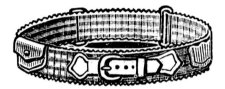

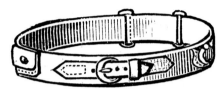

waistbands, belts and buckles • Taillenbänder, Gürtel und Schnallen • polsini, cinture e fibbie • ceintures et boucles de ceinture
pretinas, cinturones y hebillas • faixas, cintos e fivelas • ウエストバンド、ベルト、バックル • 腰帯、 皮帯和搭扣

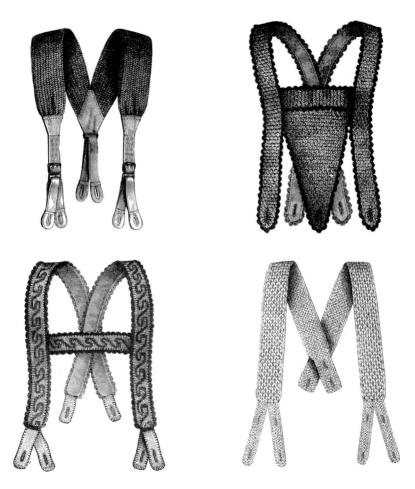

waistbands, belts and buckles • Taillenbänder, Gürtel und Schnallen • polsini, cinture e fibbie • ceintures et boucles de ceinture
pretinas, cinturones y hebillas • faixas, cintos e fivelas • ウエストバンド、ベルト、バックル • 腰带、皮带和搭扣

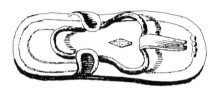

shoes and socks • Schuhe und Socken • scarpe e calze • chaussures et chaussettes • zapatos y calcetines • sapatos e meias • 靴と靴下 • 鞋袜

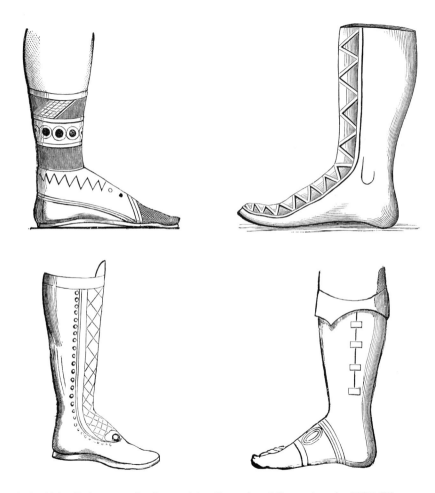

shoes and socks • Schuhe und Socken • scarpe e calze • chaussures et chaussettes • zapatos y calcetines • sapatos e meias • 靴と靴下 • 鞋袜

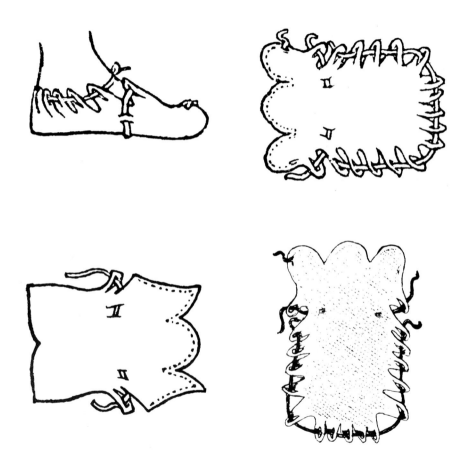

shoes and socks • Schuhe und Socken • scarpe e calze • chaussures et chaussettes • zapatos y calcetines • sapatos e meias • 靴と靴下 • 鞋袜

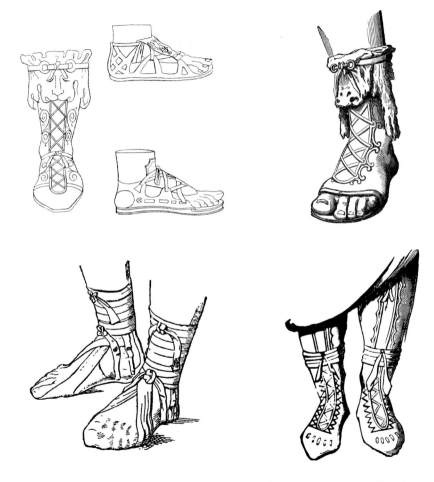

shoes and socks • Schuhe und Socken • scarpe e calze • chaussures et chaussettes • zapatos y calcetines • sapatos e meias • 靴と靴下 • 鞋袜

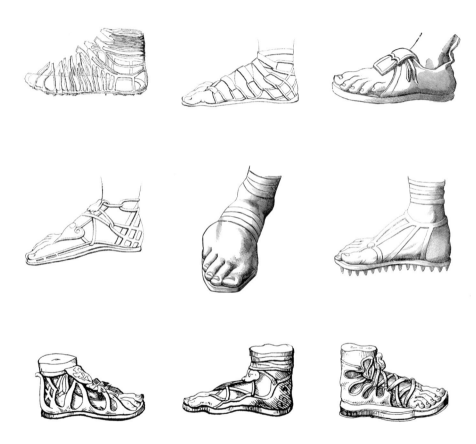

shoes and socks • Schuhe und Socken • scarpe e calze • chaussures et chaussettes • zapatos y calcetines • sapatos e meias • 靴と靴下 • 鞋袜

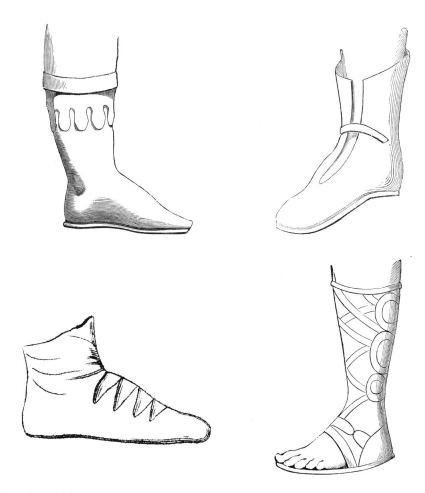

shoes and socks • Schuhe und Socken • scarpe e calze • chaussures et chaussettes • zapatos y calcetines • sapatos e meias • 靴と靴下 • 鞋袜

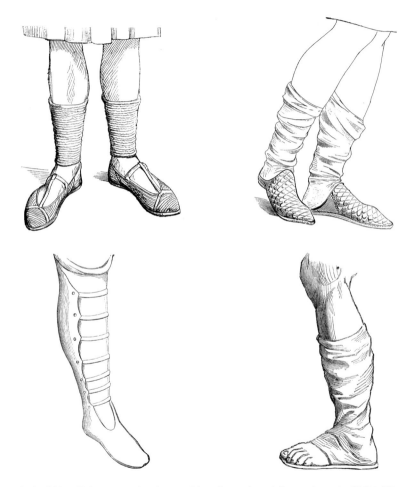

shoes and socks • Schuhe und Socken • scarpe e calze • chaussures et chaussettes • zapatos y calcetines • sapatos e meias • 靴と靴下 • 鞋袜

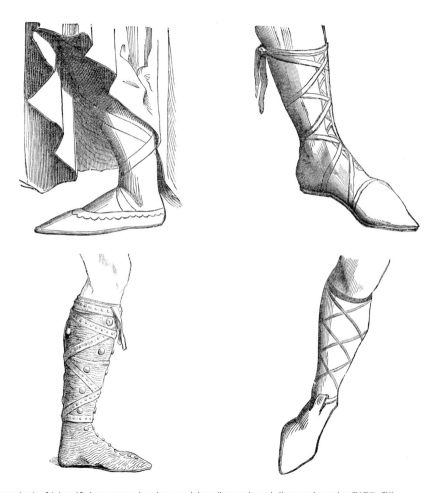

shoes and socks • Schuhe und Socken • scarpe e calze • chaussures et chaussettes • zapatos y calcetines • sapatos e meias • 靴と靴下 • 鞋袜

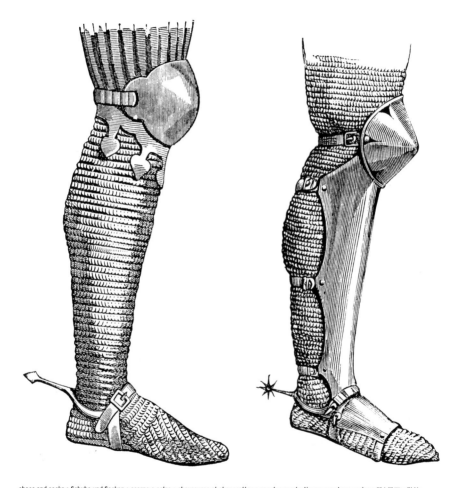

shoes and socks • Schuhe und Socken • scarpe e calze • chaussures et chaussettes • zapatos y calcetines • sapatos e meias • 靴と靴下 • 鞋袜

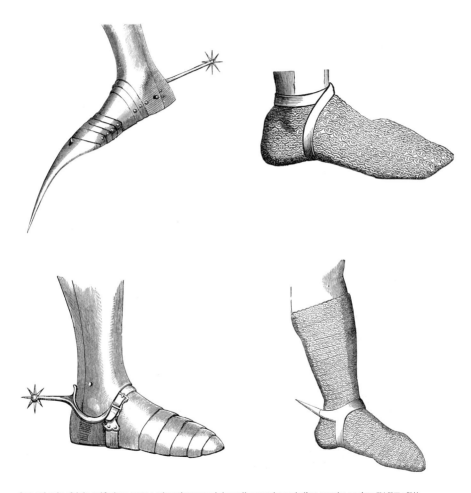

shoes and socks • Schuhe und Socken • scarpe e calze • chaussures et chaussettes • zapatos y calcetines • sapatos e meias • 靴と靴下 • 鞋袜

shoes and socks • Schuhe und Socken • scarpe e calze • chaussures et chaussettes • zapatos y calcetines • sapatos e meias • 靴と靴下 • 鞋袜

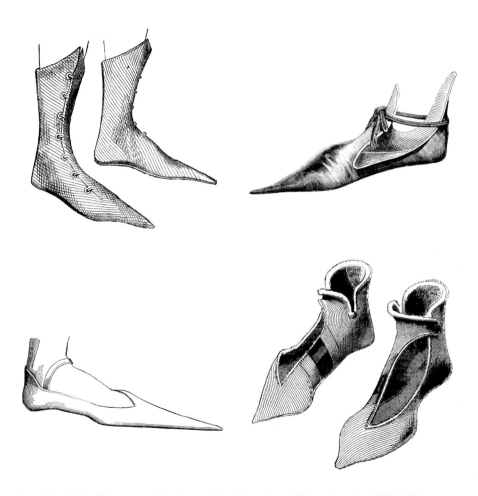

shoes and socks • Schuhe und Socken • scarpe e calze • chaussures et chaussettes • zapatos y calcetines • sapatos e meias • 靴と靴下 • 鞋袜

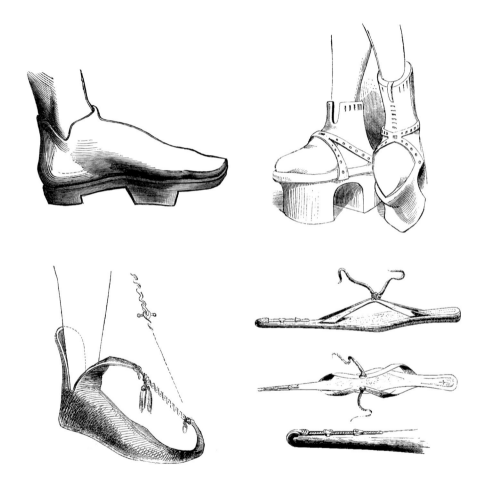

shoes and socks • Schuhe und Socken • scarpe e calze • chaussures et chaussettes • zapatos y calcetines • sapatos e meias • 靴と靴下 • 鞋袜

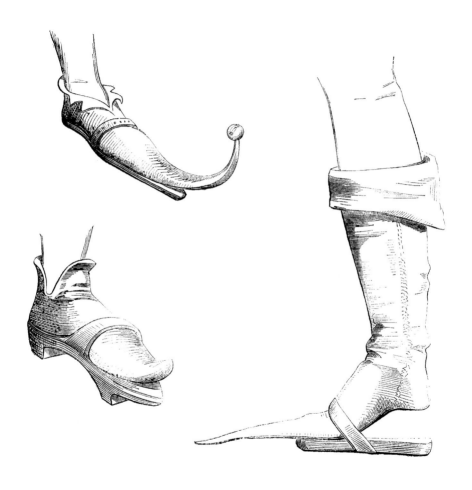

shoes and socks • Schuhe und Socken • scarpe e calze • chaussures et chaussettes • zapatos y calcetines • sapatos e meias • 靴と靴下 • 鞋袜

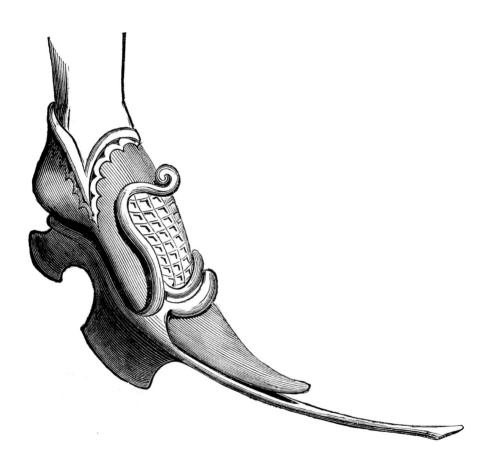

shoes and socks • Schuhe und Socken • scarpe e calze • chaussures et chaussettes • zapatos y calcetines • sapatos e meias • 靴と靴下 • 鞋袜

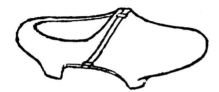

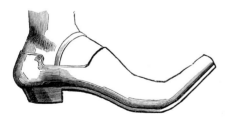

shoes and socks • Schuhe und Socken • scarpe e calze • chaussures et chaussettes • zapatos y calcetines • sapatos e meias • 靴と靴下 • 鞋袜

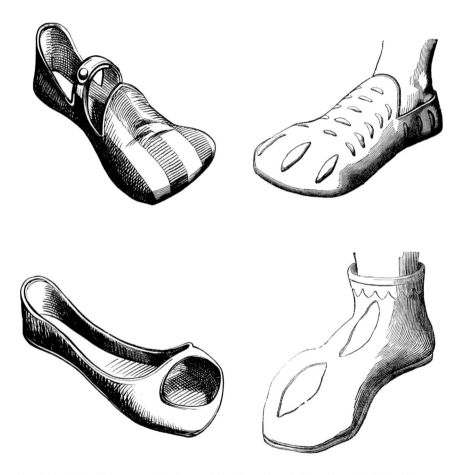

shoes and socks • Schuhe und Socken • scarpe e calze • chaussures et chaussettes • zapatos y calcetines • sapatos e meias • 靴と靴下 • 鞋袜

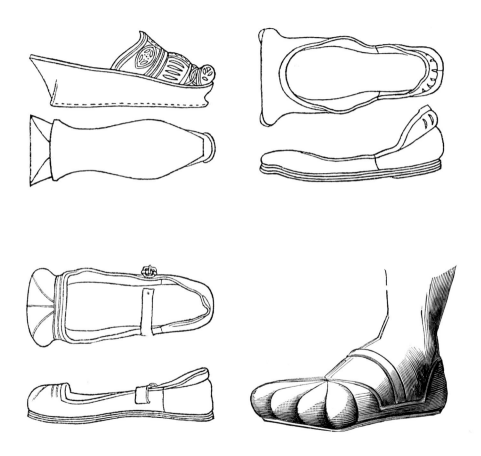

shoes and socks • Schuhe und Socken • scarpe e calze • chaussures et chaussettes • zapatos y calcetines • sapatos e meias • 靴と靴下 • 鞋袜

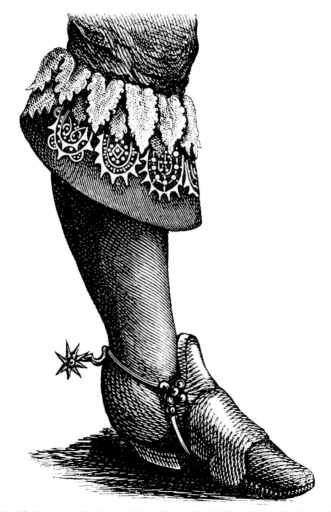

shoes and socks • Schuhe und Socken • scarpe e calze • chaussures et chaussettes • zapatos y calcetines • sapatos e meias • 靴と靴下 • 鞋袜

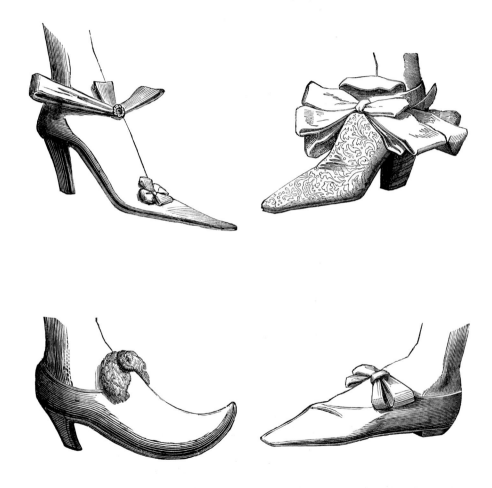

shoes and socks • Schuhe und Socken • scarpe e calze • chaussures et chaussettes • zapatos y calcetines • sapatos e meias • 靴と靴下 • 鞋袜

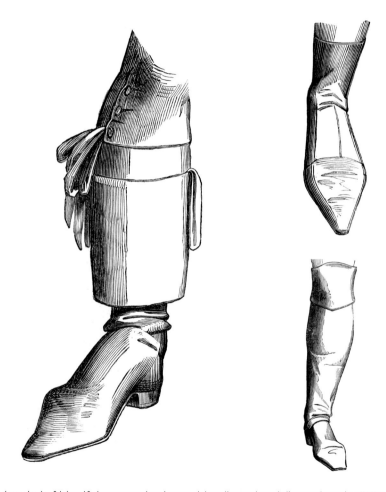

shoes and socks • Schuhe und Socken • scarpe e calze • chaussures et chaussettes • zapatos y calcetines • sapatos e meias • 靴と靴下 • 鞋袜

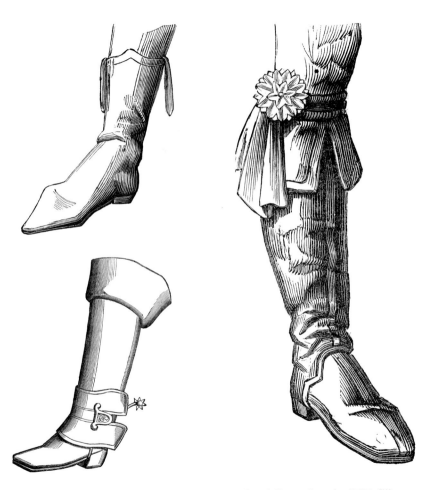

shoes and socks • Schuhe und Socken • scarpe e calze • chaussures et chaussettes • zapatos y calcetines • sapatos e meias • 靴と靴下 • 鞋袜

shoes and socks • Schuhe und Socken • scarpe e calze • chaussures et chaussettes • zapatos y calcetines • sapatos e meias • 靴と靴下 • 鞋袜

shoes and socks • Schuhe und Socken • scarpe e calze • chaussures et chaussettes • zapatos y calcetines • sapatos e meias • 靴と靴下 • 鞋袜

shoes and socks • Schuhe und Socken • scarpe e calze • chaussures et chaussettes • zapatos y calcetines • sapatos e meias • 靴と靴下 • 鞋袜

shoes and socks • Schuhe und Socken • scarpe e calze • chaussures et chaussettes • zapatos y calcetines • sapatos e meias • 靴と靴下 • 鞋袜

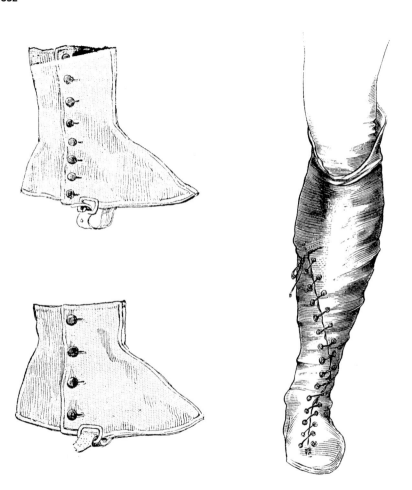

shoes and socks • Schuhe und Socken • scarpe e calze • chaussures et chaussettes • zapatos y calcetines • sapatos e meias • 靴と靴下 • 鞋袜

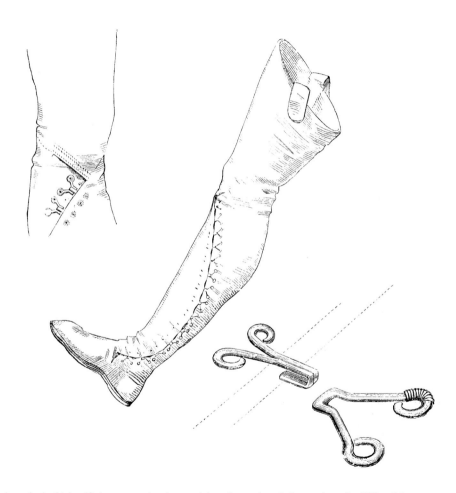

shoes and socks • Schuhe und Socken • scarpe e calze • chaussures et chaussettes • zapatos y calcetines • sapatos e meias • 靴と靴下 • 鞋袜

shoes and socks • Schuhe und Socken • scarpe e calze • chaussures et chaussettes • zapatos y calcetines • sapatos e meias • 靴と靴下 • 鞋袜

shoes and socks • Schuhe und Socken • scarpe e calze • chaussures et chaussettes • zapatos y calcetines • sapatos e meias • 靴と靴下 • 鞋袜

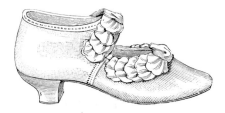

shoes and socks • Schuhe und Socken • scarpe e calze • chaussures et chaussettes • zapatos y calcetines • sapatos e meias • 靴と靴下 • 鞋袜

shoes and socks • Schuhe und Socken • scarpe e calze • chaussures et chaussettes • zapatos y calcetines • sapatos e meias • 靴と靴下 • 鞋袜

shoes and socks • Schuhe und Socken • scarpe e calze • chaussures et chaussettes • zapatos y calcetines • sapatos e meias • 靴と靴下 • 鞋袜

shoes and socks • Schuhe und Socken • scarpe e calze • chaussures et chaussettes • zapatos y calcetines • sapatos e meias • 靴と靴下 • 鞋袜

shoes and socks • Schuhe und Socken • scarpe e calze • chaussures et chaussettes • zapatos y calcetines • sapatos e meias • 靴と靴下 • 鞋袜

shoes and socks • Schuhe und Socken • scarpe e calze • chaussures et chaussettes • zapatos y calcetines • sapatos e meias • 靴と靴下 • 鞋袜

shoes and socks • Schuhe und Socken • scarpe e calze • chaussures et chaussettes • zapatos y calcetines • sapatos e meias • 靴と靴下 • 鞋袜

shoes and socks • Schuhe und Socken • scarpe e calze • chaussures et chaussettes • zapatos y calcetines • sapatos e meias • 靴と靴下 • 鞋袜

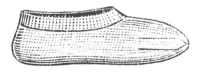

shoes and socks • Schuhe und Socken • scarpe e calze • chaussures et chaussettes • zapatos y calcetines • sapatos e meias • 靴と靴下 • 鞋袜

shoes and socks • Schuhe und Socken • scarpe e calze • chaussures et chaussettes • zapatos y calcetines • sapatos e meias • 靴と靴下 • 鞋袜

shoes and socks • Schuhe und Socken • scarpe e calze • chaussures et chaussettes • zapatos y calcetines • sapatos e meias • 靴と靴下 • 鞋袜

shoes and socks • Schuhe und Socken • scarpe e calze • chaussures et chaussettes • zapatos y calcetines • sapatos e meias • 靴と靴下 • 鞋袜

shoes and socks • Schuhe und Socken • scarpe e calze • chaussures et chaussettes • zapatos y calcetines • sapatos e meias • 靴と靴下 • 鞋袜

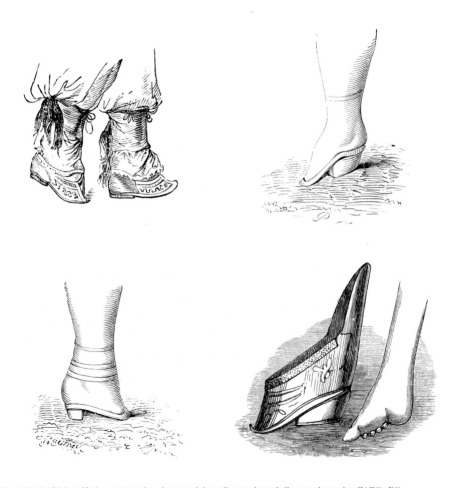

shoes and socks • Schuhe und Socken • scarpe e calze • chaussures et chaussettes • zapatos y calcetines • sapatos e meias • 靴と靴下 • 鞋袜

shoes and socks • Schuhe und Socken • scarpe e calze • chaussures et chaussettes • zapatos y calcetines • sapatos e meias • 靴と靴下 • 鞋袜

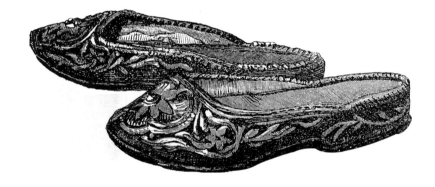

shoes and socks • Schuhe und Socken • scarpe e calze • chaussures et chaussettes • zapatos y calcetines • sapatos e meias • 靴と靴下 • 鞋袜

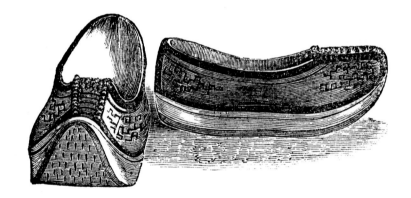

shoes and socks • Schuhe und Socken • scarpe e calze • chaussures et chaussettes • zapatos y calcetines • sapatos e meias • 靴と靴下 • 鞋袜

shoes and socks • Schuhe und Socken • scarpe e calze • chaussures et chaussettes • zapatos y calcetines • sapatos e meias • 靴と靴下 • 鞋袜

descriptions • Beschreibungen • descrizioni • descriptions • descripciones • Descrições • 説明 • 说明

380

descriptions • Beschreibungen • descrizioni • descriptions • descripciones • Descrições • 說明 • 说明

384

Page	From left to right, top to bottom
259	Chinese women with umbrellas, China, c. 1840
260	Parasols, United Kingdom, c. 1874
261	Parasols, United Kingdom, 19th century
262	A variety of parasols, United Kingdom, c. 1880
263	Decorated parasols, United Kingdom, 19th century
264	A variety of parasols, United Kingdom, c. 1880
265	A variety of parasols, United Kingdom, c. 1880
266	Lace parasol, United Kingdom, 19th century
267	Decorated parasols, United Kingdom, 19th century
268	Japanese woman with parasol and fan, Japan
269	Chinese woman fanning with fan, c. 1840
270	Chinese fan with a detail of the Summer Palace, 19th century
271	Chinese fan with decorated case, c. 1840
272	Algerian woman in housedress with fan, c. 1840
273	Egyptian woman with fan, c. 1880
274	Two servants with fan, China, c. 1900
275	Hindu priest with fan, India, c. 1860
276	Fan from Siam, 19th century
277	Fan with feathers, Indonesia, 19th century
278	Sioux woman with fan, North America, c. 1880
279	Fan made of palm leaves, 19th century Ancient Mexican fan with feathers Fan made of palm leaves, 19th century
280	Fan with feathers, 19th century
281	Fan with butterflies and feathers, 19th century Fan with feathers, 19th century Fan with feathers, 19th century Fan with feathers and butterfly, 19th century
282	Fans, 18th century
283	Lace fans, United Kingdom, c. 1880
284	Fans, United Kingdom, c. 1880
385	Fans, United Kingdom, c. 1880
286	Sword holder belonging to King Charles the Great, France, 8th century
287	Mediaeval velvet bag, France

Page	From left to right, top to bottom
287	Leather bag with three tassels , France, 15th century Leather bag , France, 15th century
288	Chinese bags worn with a belt around the waist, China, c. 1840
289	Women's bag, France, 16th century
290	Reticules, United Kingdom, c. 1870
291	Reticules, United Kingdom, c. 1870
292	Closed and open small purse made from a walnut, France, c. 1880 Ornamental purse of beads and crochet, United Kingdom, c. 1874 Knitted purse with beads, France, c. 1880
293	Knitted purses, United Kingdom, c. 1874
294	Silver chain bag with fringe and silver balls, United Kingdom, 1920s Silver pleated chain bag, United Kingdom, 1920s Knitted bag with beads, France, c. 1880 Silver chain Dorothy bag, United Kingdom, 1920s
295	Knitted bag, France, c. 1880 Bag with shell, France, c. 1880 Chatelaine bag, United Kingdom, c. 1874
296	Embroidered silk pocket, United Kingdom, c. 1874 Pocket worn around the waist, France, c. 1880 Embroidered pocket, United Kingdom, c. 1874
297	Small bag, France, c. 1880 Small pocket made of sunflower seeds, France, c. 1880 Fancy silk pocket, United Kingdom, c. 1874
298	Baskets, France, c. 1880
299	Crochet basket with silk bag, United Kingdom, c. 1874 Basket, France, c. 1880 Basket, France, c. 1880
300	Handbag, France, c. 1880 Case for travelling wraps (closed) United Kingdom, c. 1874 Rug straps, United Kingdom, 1930s
301	Case for travelling wraps (open), United Kingdom, c. 1874

388

descriptions • Beschreibungen • descrizioni • descriptions • descripciones • Descrições • 説明 • 说明

descriptions • Beschreibungen • descrizioni • descriptions • descripciones • Descrições • 説明 • 说明